# GUIDELINES FOR THE PROMOTION OF ENVIRONMENTAL MANAGEMENT OF COASTAL AQUACULTURE DEVELPOMENT

# GUIDELINES FOR THE PROMOTION OF ENVIRONMENTAL MANAGEMENT OF COASTAL AQUACULTURE DEVELPOMENT

U.C. Barg

Reprinted by arrangement with the
Food and Agriculture Organization of the United Nations

by
**Daya Publishing House**
*A Division of*
**Astral International Pvt Ltd**
**New Delhi - 110 002**

"This book was originally published by the Food and Agriculture Organization of the United Nations (FAO) as Vaccine Manual, FAO Animal Production and Health Series No. 35".


First Indian Edition, 1997
Reprinted, 2024
ISBN: 9788170351856

*Published by* : **Daya Publishing House**
A Division of
Astral International Pvt Ltd
4736/23, Ansari Road
Darya Ganj, New Delhi - 110002
Phone: 011-43549197
Email: info@astralint.com
Web: www.astralint.com

*Printed at* : **Chawla Offset Printers,**
Delhi-110 052

## PREPARATION OF THIS DOCUMENT

The Fishery Resources and Environment Division of the FAO Fisheries Department regularly publishes technical documentation relevant for the promotion of sustainable fisheries and aquaculture development. The preparation of this document has been fostered by the FAO Aquaculture Steering Committee and the FAO Inter-Departmental Working Group on Integrated Coastal Area Management. This document is for circulation to both specialists and government officials involved in the planning and management of aquaculture development in coastal areas. Comments and suggestions for improvements of the present version would be appreciated and should be sent to the Fishery Resources Officer (Aquatic Environment), Inland Water Resources and Aquaculture Service (FIRI), Fisheries Department, FAO, Rome.

The preparation of this document benefitted from discussions and suggestions by FAO Fisheries Department staff, in particular by A. Tacon, J. Kapetsky, H. Naeve, M. Pedini, P. Martosubroto, D. Insull, R. Willmann, and by A. Van Houtte (FAO Legal Office). Many individual experts as well as international organizations provided useful experience and guideline documentation. The continuous assistance and patient support by the staff of the FAO Fisheries Branch Library is greatly appreciated.

Distribution:

Directors of Fisheries and Aquaculture
FAO Regional Fishery Commissions and Working Groups
Aquaculture (Marine Water)
FAO Fisheries Department
FAO Regional Fishery Officers
FAO Inter-Departmental Working Group on Environment and Sustainable Development / Sub-Group on Integrated Coastal Area Management
National Environment Coordinators with the Network of Aquaculture Centres in Asia-Pacific (NACA) and the FAO/NACA Project TCP/RAS/2253 (Regional study and workshop on environmental assessment and management of aquaculture development)
Coastal aquaculture development projects executed by FAO
Interested international organizations and institutions

Barg, U.C.
Guidelines for the promotion of environmental management of coastal aquaculture development (based on a review of selected experiences and concepts).
FAO Fisheries Technical Paper. No. 328. Rome, FAO. 1992. 122 p.

## ABSTRACT

This document is directed to aquaculture development specialists, coastal resource use planners and government officials involved and interested in the planning and management of coastal aquaculture development within the wider context of resource use in coastal areas. It is intended to serve in the promotion of environmental management of coastal aquaculture. Guidelines are given for improved environmental management of coastal aquaculture based on an overview of selected published experiences and concepts. Potential adverse environmental effects of and on coastal aquaculture practices are addressed with consideration of main socio-economic and bio-physical factors. Methodologies are presented for the assessment and monitoring of environmental hazards and impacts of coastal aquaculture. Selected environmental management options are described for application both at policy-level and farm-level.

# TABLE OF CONTENTS

# 1. INTRODUCTION

## 1.1 Definitions and Background

FAO (1990) defined aquaculture as "the farming of aquatic organisms, including fish, molluscs, crustaceans, and aquatic plants. Farming implies some form of intervention in the rearing process to enhance production, such as regular stocking, feeding, protection from predators, etc. Farming also implies individual or corporate ownership of the stock being cultivated. For statistical purposes, aquatic organisms which are harvested by an individual or corporate body which has owned them throughout their rearing period contribute to aquaculture, while aquatic organisms which are exploitable by the public as a common property resource, with or without appropriate licenses, are the harvest of fisheries."

For the purposes of this document, the geographical area covered by the term "coastal" includes the shoreland influenced by the sea, the water column and the seabed extending to edge of the continental shelf (Sorensen and McCreary, 1990). Hence, the term "coastal aquaculture" covers land-based and water-based brackish and marine aquaculture practices.

Aquaculture production is increasing worldwide, and it is expected that aquaculture activities will be expanding significantly in the near future as practices are further improved and diversified. Aquaculture production in 1990 constituted approximately 15.3% of the world's fishery production (see FAO, 1992) as compared to 14% in 1989 (New, 1991; see also FAO, 1991a). Coastal aquaculture production in 1990 amounted to approximately 7.5 million metric tons estimated to be worth US$ 13 230 million (see FAO, 1992). Driving forces in aquaculture development are the increasing demand for aquaculture produce, generating profit and income, and the urgent need for sustainable food supply.

Aquaculture interacts with the environment. It utilizes resources and causes environmental changes. Most interactions have beneficial effects. There have been substantial socio-economic benefits arising from the expansion of aquaculture. These benefits include increased income, employment, foreign exchange earnings and improved nutrition (Pullin, 1989). It should be recognized that to date the majority of aquaculture practices have had little adverse effect on ecosystems. Nevertheless, some cases of environmental degradation in coastal areas have occurred due to, for example, intensive cage culture operations in Europe and shrimp farming practices in Southeast Asia and Latin America.

Aquaculture operations in many temperate and tropical countries still can be improved. Current aquaculture development efforts need to be strengthened to further improve the management and operation of many aquafarms to ensure their durability and environmental compatibility. Unfortunately, the planning and coordination of aquaculture development supported by an appropriate information base containing sufficient technological and socio-economic data is still an exception rather than common practice in most countries.

Although there is potential for development in many areas, aquaculture may increasingly be subject to a range of environmental, resource and market constraints. Aquaculture is competing for land and water resources, which in some cases resulted in conflicts with other resource users. Also, there is growing concern about the environmental implications of aquaculture development, comprising the adverse effects of aquaculture operations on the environment as well as the consequences of increasing aquatic pollution affecting feasibility and sustainable development of aquaculture.

During the last two decades, increasing attention has been directed toward the potential environmental hazards associated with aquaculture development. In some cases, environmental problems have resulted from conversion of wetland habitats, nutrient and organic waste discharges, introduction of exotic species, chemical usage, as well as from deterioration of water quality and decreasing availability of suitable sites for aquaculture. These problems have been repeatedly addressed at international expert consultations, for example, by the Indo-Pacific Fishery Commission (IPFC), the European Inland Fisheries Advisory Commission (EIFAC), the International Council for the Exploration of the Sea (ICES), the Asian Fisheries Society, the International Center for Living Aquatic Resources Management (ICLARM), the World Aquaculture Society (WAS), the European Aquaculture Society (EAS) and the IMO/FAO/Unesco/WMO/WHO/IAEA/UN/UNEP[1] Joint Group of Experts on the Scientific Aspects of Marine Pollution (GESAMP).

Recommendations from these consultations repeatedly emphasized the urgent need for improvements in various fields including (i) application of appropriate aquaculture methods, (ii) sectoral development planning and management, (iii) integration of aquaculture in multi-sectoral coastal area and river basin management frameworks, (iv) legislation governing aquaculture, and (v) assessment and monitoring of ecological and socio-economic changes associated with aquaculture developments.

### 1.2 Purpose and Scope of this Document

This document is intended to assist in the promotion of environmental management of coastal aquaculture. It is addressed to all those who are involved and interested in the planning, development and management of environmentally-acceptable coastal aquaculture. It is also intended to serve experts pursuing environmental management and development in coastal areas.

General guidelines are given for environmental management of coastal aquaculture development based on an overview of relevant published information currently available. These guidelines, as formulated in Section 2, directly refer the reader to the relevant sections of the overview containing more specific background and guidance information (Sections 3-6). It is hoped, that, by providing relevant reference material to the guidelines presented, this document proves useful in improving formulation and implementation of appropriate country-specific approaches and actions to meet the particular ecological and socio-economic circumstances governing coastal aquaculture development.

In Section 3 it has been attempted to outline the environmental implications of coastal aquaculture development in the wider context of the utilization of coastal resources and related concomitant environmental changes. Further, main bio-physical and socio-economic factors and causes for environmental deterioration and mismanagement specific to coastal aquaculture are addressed in order to highlight possible constraints to environment-compatible development (Section 4). Methodologies are presented for the assessment and monitoring of environmental hazards and impacts of coastal aquaculture (Section 5). Selected environmental management options are described for possible application both at policy-level and farm-level (Section 6).

Much effort has been made to focus on environmental and developmental

---

[1] **IMO**: International Maritime Organization; **FAO**: Food and Agriculture Organization of the United Nations; **Unesco**: United Nations Educational, Scientific and Cultural Organization; **WMO**: World Meteorological Organization; **WHO**: World Health Organization; **IAEA**: International Atomic Energy Agency; **UN**: United Nations; **UNEP**: United Nations Environment Programme.

circumstances and requirements of coastal aquaculture practices in developing countries. Unfortunately, there is a substantial lack of adequate information and data related to adverse environmental effects of coastal aquaculture in developing countries. Furthermore, information available from temperate countries in most cases cannot be used to quantitatively assess or predict adverse environmental effects of aquacultural practices in tropical environments. Also, much of the concerns so far formulated on the potential adverse effects of aquaculture are still of a speculative nature, and are not borne out by scientific evidence (Pillay, 1992). The paucity of adequate research specific to the different aquaculture practices and their distinct environmental settings makes definitive judgements extremely difficult.

All guideline documentations carry limitations due to both their general character and broad scope. In view of the variety of coastal aquaculture practices and the diversity of their environmental settings found worldwide, it is likely that some of the issues addressed in this document would have needed more detailed elaboration to meet the specific and possibly differing information requirements various readers might have. The readers are therefore encouraged to comment on this document and to make suggestions for its improvement possibly by indicating the specific environmental and developmental circumstances facilitating or restricting progress in coastal aquaculture in their countries or projects.

Environmental management of coastal aquaculture development, and its promotion is a challenging task. Coastal aquaculture is very diverse in terms of the people involved, the resources used, the various methods applied, and, regarding the environmental characteristics of existing and potential sites. Thus, there are opportunities for improved adaptation and integration of aquaculture practices into coastal area development processes. It is believed that appropriate environmental management of aquaculture in coastal areas can be achieved by strengthening efforts towards increased success and efficiency in the development and management of aquaculture operations.

## 2. GUIDELINES FOR THE PROMOTION OF ENVIRONMENTAL MANAGEMENT OF COASTAL AQUACULTURE DEVELOPMENT

The ecological and socio-economic benefits and costs of aquaculture activities are potentially so significant that policies are necessary to ensure that financial gain is not at the expense of the ecosystem or the rest of society; aquaculture developments should follow established principles and policies. The following general principles and policies are proposed (adapted from GESAMP, 1991c):

### 2.1 General Principles

- Coastal aquaculture has the potential to produce food and generate income contributing to social and economic well-being.

- Planned and properly managed aquaculture development is a productive use of coastal areas which should be undertaken within the broader framework of integrated coastal area management plans, according to national economic objectives and national goals for sustainable development and in harmony with international obligations.

- The likely adverse consequences of aquaculture and other coastal developments on the social and ecological environment must be predicted and evaluated, and measures formulated in order to contain these consequences within acceptable, pre-determined limits.

- Aquaculture and other activities in coastal areas should be adequately regulated and monitored to ensure that adverse effects remain within pre-determined limits and to detect when contingency and other plans need to be brought into effect to reverse any trends which could lead toward unacceptable environmental consequences.

### 2.2 Policies

- The sound utilization of the ecological capacity of the coastal area to produce aquatic products and generate income.

- The development of policy and management mechanisms to reduce conflict with other coastal activities.

- The prevention or reduction of the adverse environmental impacts of coastal aquaculture and other coastal activities.

- The management and coordination of aquaculture activities to ensure that their adverse impacts remain within acceptable limits.

- The reduction of health risks from the consumption of aquaculture products.

### 2.3 Actions

There is a variety of activities which can be undertaken to promote environmental management of coastal aquaculture and to achieve its successful development. The following actions are suggested:

(Specific background and guidance information related to the actions suggested below is provided in the overview sections 3-6 beginning on page 11. The actions are grouped below as related to these sections. The paragraphs in the overview sections are numbered, starting on page 11. For more details on each action proposed, please see relevant paragraphs.)

## • *Coastal aquaculture and the environment: understanding the context*
(Section 3 refers)

1. Emphasize the socio-economic and ecological benefits of coastal aquaculture. Collect and provide information on opportunities and achievements in coastal aquaculture development.
(see paragraphs 2-6)

2. Enhance awareness and understanding of the potential adverse environmental effects of coastal aquaculture. Address both the bio-physical and socio-economic aspects of environmental interactions associated with coastal aquaculture activities.
(paragraphs 7-78)

3. Distinguish between the species cultured, the farming methods applied and the prevailing ecological characteristics of the aquaculture site. Most scientific evidence on adverse ecological impact due to aquaculture originates from temperate countries and cannot be applied to aquaculture in tropical environments. Encourage research on ecological interactions of coastal aquaculture.
(paragraphs 17-60)

4. Emphasize the risks of self-pollution and other negative feedback effects. In particular, address the self-pollution risks of increasing aggregation of aquafarms in coastal embayments.
(paragraphs 61-66)

5. Consider aquaculture as one of many activities in coastal areas. Multiple resource use in coastal areas in many cases results in serious pollution of coastal waters. Highlight possible threats to aquaculture due to increasing pollution in coastal areas.
(paragraphs 67-72; see also Annex 2)

6. Address potential negative social implications of aquaculture and other developments, in particular human health risks, resource use conflicts and possible marginalization of low-income groups.
(paragraphs 73-78)

## • *Defining factors influencing environmental performance of coastal aquaculture*
(Section 4 refers)

7. Determine the factors affecting environmental compatibility of coastal aquaculture in your project or country. Specify causes of environmental mismanagement and constraints to sustainable development of coastal aquaculture. Describe ecological, biological and technological circumstances as well as socio-economic, institutional and legal conditions relevant for coastal aquaculture development.
(paragraphs 79-91; see also 215, 225; 227-229; 237-238; 254)

## • *Assessing environmental hazards and impacts of coastal aquaculture*
(Section 5 refers)

8. **Assess the capacity of the coastal ecosystem to sustain aquaculture development with minimal ecological change.**
(paragraphs 93-153)

→ *Pollution assessment / monitoring methods*

9. **Promote understanding of the environmental capacity concept. Encourage application of modern scientific methodologies for the assessment of coastal pollution such as the hazard assessment approach and adequate monitoring schemes. Advocate the establishment of a cooperative early detection/warning network of fishermen and aquaculturists.**
(paragraphs 95-103 and 104-113; 112)

10. **Apply, where possible, pollution assessment methods which are specific to coastal aquaculture. Ensure appropriate use of these methods, based on proper understanding of their applicability and limitations. Encourage further development of assessment methods suitable to aquaculture practices and ecological conditions in tropical environments.**
(paragraphs 114-143)

11. **Integrate aquaculture-specific monitoring schemes into existing coastal water pollution assessment activities. Select appropriate monitoring parameters and suitable sampling stations.**
(paragraphs 148-153; see also Annex 4)

12. **Employ remote sensing techniques and geographical information systems (GIS) to assess large-scale spatial and temporal environmental changes due to aquaculture and other developments in coastal areas.**
(paragraphs 146-147)

→ *Implementation of environmental impact assessment (EIA)*

13. **Enhance awareness on advantages and limitations associated with the implementation of environmental impact assessment (EIA) concepts.**
(paragraphs 154-170)

14. **Consider that assessment studies on the social and economic impact of development activities may be carried out separately or as an integral part of an EIA. Both types of impact assessments are essential when formulating coastal aquaculture programmes and projects.**
(paragraphs 155-156; see also 233-236 and 240-241)

15. **Select or adapt an appropriate EIA sequence according to prevalent environmental and development requirements and according to the availability of information and implementation capacities.**
(paragraphs 157-167)

16. **Apply the EIA process to all major coastal aquaculture development proposals. Provide information to applicants/developers on options for mitigatory and adaptive measures to be included in project proposals.**
(paragraphs 157-164; see also 177-178, 181; 218-223 and 242-278)

17. **Incorporate EIA into integrated coastal area management strategies.**
(paragraphs 168-170; see also 206-207)

## ● *Improving environmental management of coastal aquaculture development*

(Section 6 refers)

18. **Select and implement environmental management options which suit the specific requirements for environmentally-acceptable development of aquaculture and other activities in coastal areas.**
(paragraphs 171-278)

→ *Environment protection*

19. **Improve/develop management processes for protection of coastal environments.**
(paragraphs 173-189; see also 236 and Annex 3)

→ *Integrated coastal area management (ICAM)*

20. **Join efforts with other coastal resource managers to formulate (or improve) and implement integrated coastal area management (ICAM) plans. There is a broad array of possible institutional arrangements and management strategies to resolve coastal use conflicts and manage coastal resources. Contribute to the establishment of an institutionalized coordination office or cooperation network.**
(paragraphs 190-214; see also Annex 7)

21. **Encourage broad participation in development and implementation of coastal programmes and coastal area management. Aquafarmers, artisanal and other resource users, the scientific community, and non-governmental organizations should participate or be consulted, as appropriate, in ICAM activities, along with representatives of key government bureaux who have a stake in coastal management.**
(paragraphs 196-197; 214)

22. **Coastal aquaculture development planners should actively participate in the formulation and implementation of ICAM plans. State goals and set priorities for coastal aquaculture development. Identify existing and potential coastal resource use conflicts between aquafarmers and other coastal resource users.**
(paragraphs 226, 234; 195-197)

23. **Provide aquaculture-specific data for the information base required for ICAM.**
(paragraphs 198-199; see also Annex 8)

24. **Participate in zoning activities leading to the designation of coastal resources and space. Indicate coastal areas appropriate or desired for aquaculture development possibly based on aquaculture-specific site selection surveys.**
(paragraphs 200-208; 234)

25. **Communicate frequently with other coastal resource planners and managers, stakeholder, scientists and policy-makers. Use conflict resolution techniques such as facilitated policy dialogues and mediated negotiation.**
(paragraph 209)

26. **Help to ensure long-term funding for ICAM, through durable commitment of parties involved in aquaculture and their enforcement of aquaculture-specific regulations adopted.**
(paragraphs 210-214)

→ *Legal framework*

27. **Promote the formulation of a flexible and specific legal framework in support of aquaculture development. Help to provide and enforce environmental legislation which is formulated with due account of the variety of aquaculture practices and diversity of environmental settings.**
(paragraphs 215-225)

28. **Environmental legislation should ensure accessibility and environmental protection of areas and resources required for coastal aquaculture development.**
(paragraphs 218; see also 208, 214 and 236)

29. **Contribute to the formulation of constructive environmental regulations for coastal aquaculture, where necessary, such as requirements for EIA, waste discharge limits and waste treatment specifications. Apply incentives and deterrents to reduce existing environmental degradation from aquaculture activities.**
(paragraphs 219-222; see also Annex 3)

30. **Adopt and apply the EIFAC/ICES codes of practice on introductions and transfers of marine and freshwater organisms. Movement of species from and to aquaculture sites should be controlled through inspection and certification.**
(paragraph 223)

31. **Coastal aquaculture products should conform with safety standards for seafood before they are offered for human consumption. Establish quality control measures for aquaculture products. Control the use of aquaculture chemicals such as antibiotics and pesticides.**
(paragraph 224; see also 260-267; 268-278)

→ *Planning and management of coastal aquaculture development*

32. **Formulate/improve coastal aquaculture development and management plans.**
(paragraphs 226-238)

33. **Strengthen sectoral capacities for adequate coordination of coastal aquaculture development efforts.**
(paragraph 227)

34. **Co-operate with national development planners to ensure proper integration of coastal aquaculture development objectives and plans into national economic and agricultural development programmes.**
(paragraph 231)

35. **Emphasis should be given to compatibility of policies and plans aiming at the development of aquaculture and other sectors as well as environmental protection.**
(paragraphs 233-236)

36. **Help to ensure continuous and well-targeted support to coastal aquaculture development.**
(paragraphs 237-238)

→ *Environmental farm management*

37. Promote environmental management at farm or project level. Consult with aquafarmers on specific environmental problems and mitigatory measures adopted. Provide opportunities for exchange of related experiences. Provide information and training to aquafarmers on options for improved environmental farm management. (paragraphs 239-278)

38. Improve current aquaculture practices in terms of adequate site selection, efficiency in farm operation and maintenance, and continuous monitoring of biological and hygienic conditions on the farm. Avoid over-stocking. (paragraph 239)

39. Formulate coastal aquaculture projects which are environmentally acceptable. (paragraphs 240-241)

→→ *Use of mangrove wetland*

40. Discourage, where possible, the use of pristine mangrove wetland for aquaculture. Provide instructions governing the use of mangrove wetlands. (paragraphs 243-245)

→→ *Waste management*

41. Encourage the development of low-cost waste treatment technology for use in intensive land-based coastal aquaculture in developing countries. (paragraphs 246-247)

42. Promote integrated polyculture practices to reduce waste loadings. (paragraph 248)

43. Explore ecological and economic feasibility of site rotation. (paragraphs 249, 251)

→→ *Use of feeds and fertilizers*

44. Improve on-farm feed management practices. Improve fertilization and feeding strategies. Avoid over-use of fertilizers and feeds. (paragraphs 252-259)

45. Continue research efforts on pond metabolism. Encourage development of diets and feeding methods adapted to requirements of semi-intensive farming systems in developing countries. (paragraphs 253-254)

46. Encourage adoption of feeding regimes adjusted to specific feeding habits and behaviour of the species cultured with due consideration of water quality and water movements in the farming unit. Monitoring of feed application and, where possible, feeding response of cultured stock is essential. (paragraphs 255-257)

47. Continue efforts to improve physical and nutritional properties of manufactured feeds for use in both warmwater and coldwater aquaculture. Special emphasis should be given to applied research on dietary nutrient requirements of warmwater fish and shrimp species. (paragraphs 258-259; 254)

→→ *Use of chemicals*

48. Avoid usage of hazardous chemical substances. Emphasize measures to prevent water-quality deterioration, disease outbreaks and pests. Detailed on-farm record keeping on chemical usage is essential.
(paragraphs 260-267; 261-262; 266)

49. Discourage prophylactic use of antibiotics. Reduce environmental risks through minimal and alternating application of drugs.
(paragraph 263)

50. Establish, where needed, aquaculture health management services to cover requirements for quarantine, diagnosis, treatment, monitoring and product quality control.
(paragraphs 264-265)

51. Control market availability of potentially hazardous chemicals through consent mechanisms, e.g., registration and licensing. Aquafarmers must be provided with comprehensive information on environmental risks and appropriate use of chemicals.
(paragraph 267)

→→ *Contamination of aquaculture products*

52. Promote further development of economically viable methods for depuration/sanitation of contaminated shellfish products. Monitor contaminant levels in shellfish grown in areas subject to pollution and blooms of toxic algae.
(paragraphs 268-275)

53. Prepare contingency plans for aquaculture areas threatened by events of harmful algal blooms, and advise aquafarmers on possible countermeasures to reduce risks of damage to cultured stock.
(paragraph 277)

54. Promote aquaculture production in unpolluted waters and low risk areas. Increase public awareness of the safety aspects of consuming seafood. Apply, where unavoidable, temporary bans on harvesting or marketing of contaminated shellfish.
(paragraph 278)

## 3. COASTAL AQUACULTURE AND THE ENVIRONMENT: THE CONTEXT

1. Aquaculture interacts with the environment. It utilizes resources and causes environmental changes. Most interactions have beneficial effects. In this section a brief overview follows on the benefits and on the potential adverse effects of coastal aquaculture (see sub-sections 3.1 and 3.2). Coastal pollution implications for coastal aquaculture are then considered (3.3). Last, social implications of coastal aquaculture development are highlighted (3.4).

### 3.1 Benefits of Coastal Aquaculture

2. Generally, the socio-economic benefits arising from aquaculture expansion include the provision of food, contributing to improved nutrition and health, the generation of income and employment, the diversification of primary production, and, increasingly important for developing countries, foreign exchange earnings through export of high-value products (UNDP/Norway/FAO, 1987; Schmidt, 1982).

3. Aquaculture is also being promoted for its potential to compensate for the low growth rate of capture fisheries. Stocking and release of hatchery-reared organisms into inland and coastal waters support culture-based fisheries (Larkin, 1991).

4. Sustainable development of aquaculture can contribute to the prevention and control of aquatic pollution since it relies essentially on good-quality water resources.

5. Culture of molluscs and seaweeds may in certain cases counteract processes of nutrient and organic enrichment in eutrophic waters. Conversely, productivity of oligotrophic waters may be enhanced due to the nutrient and organic wastes released from aquaculture farms.

6. Aquaculture can contribute to rehabilitation of rural areas through re-use of degraded land.

### 3.2 Potential Adverse Effects of Coastal Aquaculture

7. After a short description of the key areas of ecological concern (GESAMP, 1991c; Weston, 1991; Gowen *et al.*, 1990; UNEP, 1990a; Pullin, 1989; Rosenthal *et al.*, 1988), the main potential adverse effects of the farming of seaweed, shellfish and fish are addressed (Braaten and Hektoen, 1991; Pillay, 1990; Chua *et al.*, 1989; Baluyut, 1989; Iwama, 1991).

#### 3.2.1 Key areas of ecological concern

Nutrient and organic enrichment

8. Many aquaculture operations invariably result in the release of metabolic waste products (faeces, pseudo-faeces and excreta) and uneaten food into the aquatic environment. In general, the recipient for soluble waste is the water column and the recipient for the organic waste is the sediment.

9. The release of soluble inorganic nutrients (nitrogen and phosphorus) has the potential to cause nutrient enrichment (hypernutrification) possibly followed by eutrophication (increase of primary production) of a waterbody. Related changes in phytoplankton ecology may result in algal blooms, which can be harmful to wild and farmed organisms. However, there is no evidence that algal blooms have been caused by coastal aquaculture.

10. The largest proportion of solid wastes released, which is predominantly organic carbon and nitrogen, settles to the seabed in the immediate vicinity of the farm. Organic enrichment of the benthic ecosystem may result in increased oxygen consumption by the sediment and formation of

anoxic sediments, with, in extreme cases, outgassing of carbon dioxide, methane and hydrogen sulphide; enhanced remineralization of organic nitrogen and reduction in macrofauna biomass, abundance and species composition.

11. There is evidence of very localized effects of reduced concentrations of dissolved oxygen in bottom and surface waters close to farm sites which are due to the considerable biochemical oxygen demand of released organic wastes and the respiratory demands of the cultured stock.

Degradation of wetland habitats

12. Coastal wetlands such as mangrove swamps are amongst the most productive ecosystems sustaining the ecological integrity and productivity of adjacent coastal waters, and are important breeding and nursery grounds for many commercially exploited fish and shellfish species. Several tropical countries have lost extensive mangrove areas due to clearing and conversion to fish and shrimp ponds, often accompanied by salinization and acidification of soils and aquifers.

Use of chemicals

13. A variety of chemicals are used in coastal aquaculture. These include: therapeutants, disinfectants, anaesthetics, biocides, hormones and growth promoters to control predators, prevent and control diseases and parasites and to alter sex, productive viability and growth of cultured organisms. Current concerns centre on: the longevity of bioactive compounds in animal tissues, the fate and effect of these compounds or their residues in the aquatic environment (e.g., toxicity to non-target organisms) and the stimulation of antibiotic resistance in microbial communities.

Biological interactions

14. The introduction and transfer of species and breeds for aquaculture purposes may alter or impoverish the biodiversity and genetic resources of the marine ecosystem through interbreeding, predation, competition, habitat destruction and, possibly, through the transmission of parasites and diseases.

15. Large-scale cultivation of bivalves in coastal embayments can interact with the marine food web by substantial removal of phytoplankton and organic detritus, as well as by competing with other planktonic herbivores.

16. Diseases may occur since many aquaculture practices and conditions around aquaculture operations can be stressful to the farmed stock. Stress increases susceptibility and predisposition to infectious diseases. Certain water quality conditions enhance virulence of potential pathogens. In the presence of stress and the appropriate pathogen, disease outbreaks can ensue. It has however been particularly difficult to show clearly that pathogens have been transmitted between cultured and wild organisms (Iwama, 1991; Baluyut, 1991).

### 3.2.2 Potential ecological effects of farming systems

17. It is useful to distinguish between extensive, semi-intensive and intensive farming systems when considering environmental effects of particular aquaculture operations. In extensive systems, cultured organisms are kept at low densities and may occasionally receive additional nutrition through fertilization. In semi-intensive aquaculture, cultured organisms are kept at higher densities than in extensive systems. The culture media are often fertilized and supplementary feed may be provided. In intensive aquaculture, cultured organisms are kept at high densities and feeding is regular, usually in the form of specially prepared/manufactured feeds. **Figure 1** illustrates the relative contribution of natural food organisms and artificial feeds in the nutritional budget of fish and shrimp within extensive, semi-intensive and intensive farming systems (Tacon, in press).

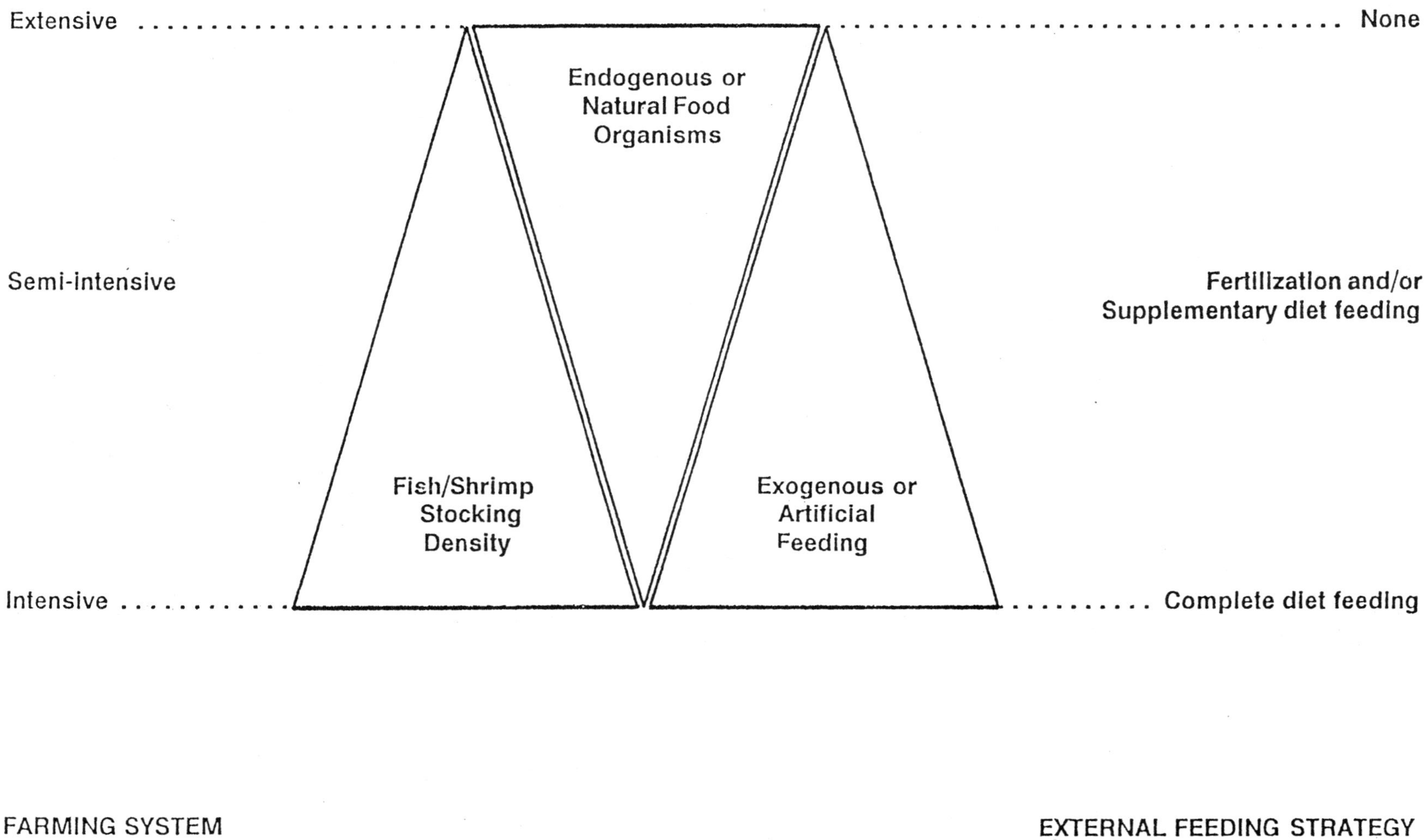


**Figure 1**: The relative contribution of natural food organisms and artificial feeds in the nutritional budget of fish and shrimp within extensive, semi-intensive and intensive farming systems (from Tacon, in press).

Seaweed culture

18. Seaweeds, being autotrophic organisms, are at the lowest trophic level of the aquatic ecosystem; they remove nutrients from the water and produce dissolved oxygen in the daytime, but consume oxygen during the night. Seaweeds are farmed (Trono, 1986, 1990; Wu, 1990; Llana, 1991; Santelices and Doty, 1989; Bird, 1989; Tseng, 1987) in shallow nearshore waters using lines, nets which are either fixed to the bottom or attached to floating rafts and buoys. Increasingly, some seaweeds are also being farmed in land-based ponds, tanks and raceways.

19. The main potential effects of sea-based systems (see **Tables 1 and 2**) probably stem from the large surface areas required for viable seaweed culture, possibly affecting benthic communities and primary productivity in the water column (Phillips, 1990). Sedimentation of organic matter from off-bottom culture units may also result in changes in benthic communities, particularly where water current velocity has been decreasing.

20. So far, there is no reported evidence on ecological impacts of chemicals being used to remove fouling organisms and predators and to control diseases, such as for example p-aminobenzene sulphonic acid, chlorox or paraquat applied in *Porphyra* and *Gracilaria* culture (Chen, 1991). Inorganic fertilizers and, occasionally, organic manure, are applied to compensate for nutrient depletion. Fertilization of *Laminaria* culture in China has resulted in enhanced production of phytoplankton and invertebrates in the culture zones (UNDP/FAO, 1989).

21. There is also concern on the negative effects of transportation of seaweed species from one region to another. Inadvertently, *Sargassum muticum* has been introduced from Japan to Europe, where it has spread to the extent of causing significant problems to navigation in some areas (Rueness, 1989).

Bivalve culture

22. Bivalves, being sedentary organisms, require substrate for spat settlement and subsequent growth, during which time they filter-feed on phytoplankton, detritus, protozoans and bacteria. Culture of oysters, mussels, clams, cockles, scallops relies on naturally available phytoplankton and requires considerable acreage of intertidal areas and nearshore waters. Bivalves are cultured both on and off the bottom using a variety of substrates such as shells, tiles, stakes, ropes, trays, floating racks, rafts, etc. (Nash, 1991; Dore, 1991; Perez Camacho *et al.,* 1991; Angell, 1991; Lovatelli, 1990; Cai and Li, 1990; Chew, 1989; Sitoy, 1988).

23. Large-scale cultivation of bivalves will consume substantial quantities of phytoplankton, particularly when there is a high density of culture units over a large area. This may show the effect of reduction of primary productivity in coastal embayments. In Japan, the culture of 50 000-60 000 oysters reduced the amount of seston (predominantly phytoplankton) by 76-95%. Suspended culture of green mussels in New Zealand was shown to remove up to 60% of the available food as the water flows through the farm, so primary production from an area many times that of the actual farm may be required to sustain maximum growth of farmed mussels (Hickmann, 1989). A mussel culture raft in the Spanish rias removes 35-40% of plankton and detritus (Figueras, 1989), whereby 30% of the carbon, 42% of the nitrogen, and 60% of the chlorophyll *a* of the particulate organic matter present in the water is retained (Perez Camacho *et al.,* 1991). However, it has also been suggested that primary productivity may be stimulated by an increase in the rate of nutrient cycling (Rosenthal *et al.,* 1988) although field evidence of increased primary production in the vicinity of farms is lacking. Bivalve culture competes with other planktonic herbivores which has been shown for the Spanish Ria de Arousa where suspended mussel culture replaced copepods as the main pelagic grazing organism.

24. Bivalve culture structures modify current velocity and direction of water movements. In turn, these changes may alter patterns of erosion and sedimentation of particulate matter. Reduced water flow may result in decrease of natural erosion by wave action, which in turn is followed by

**Table 1**: Potential physical issues associated with seaweed culture indicating their potential positive and negative effects (from Phillips, 1990).

| OPERATION AND ISSUES | POSITIVE EFFECTS | NEGATIVE EFFECTS |
|---|---|---|
| Cleaning and preparation of culture areas<br>* > * * | Improved production and management | Potential loss of native species and habitat diversity |
| Routine management (weeding, harvesting)<br>* > * * | As above | As above |
| Shading by growing seaweed<br>* > * * | Reduced competition | Reduced water column and benthic production |
| Attenuation of waves and water currents<br>* > * * * | Shelter for sensitive species | Increased sedimentation |
| Aesthetic issues<br>* > * * * | Enhanced coastal productivity in degraded ecosystems | User conflicts<br><br>Loss of resource value |
| Space<br>* > * * * | Enhanced productivity of barren or degraded ecosystems | User conflicts (e.g., with fishermen) |
| Substrate area and volume<br>* > * * * | Enhanced productivity of barren or degraded ecosystems | Ecosystem changes |

* = minimal effects
* * = potential for significant effects

**Table 2**: Ecological issues and seaweed culture, indicating their potential positive and negative effects (from Phillips, 1990).

| OPERATION AND ISSUE | POSITIVE EFFECTS | NEGATIVE EFFECTS |
|---|---|---|
| Water quality<br>* > * * | Enhanced oxygen, removal of nutrients, seaweed production | Reduced coastal phytoplankton<br><br>Nutrient cycling<br><br>"Diseases" |
| Fertilization and chemical treatments<br>* > * * | Seaweed production<br><br>Enhanced polyculture production | Product quality<br><br>Water quality changes |
| Benthos<br>* > * * | Enhanced polyculture production (e.g., with mollusc) | Changes in benthic species and production |
| Water column productivity<br>* > * * * | Enhanced production of invertebrates and finfish<br><br>Shelter of fish fry<br><br>Polyculture | Predators<br>Changes in community structure |

* = minimal effects
* * = potential for significant effects

siltation and accumulation of suspended matter in cultured areas.

25. In addition to these physical effects, bivalves produce pseudofaeces and faeces (termed biodeposition) which constitute organic-rich particulate waste from bivalve culture. For example, in Hiroshima Bay a raft holding 420 000 oysters generates 16 metric tons of faeces and pseudofaeces over a 9-month growing season, which may - with about 1 000 rafts in operation - have a major impact on sediment deposition in the bay. Culture of oysters on tables in France recorded outputs of 7.6-99 g C/m$^2$/day, depending on season and plankton production. In Sweden, sediment deposition beneath a 100-t mussel operation was estimated to be 7 kg dry matter/m$^2$ (equivalent to 1 kg C/m$^2$) during a farming period of 1.5-2 years which was due to a sedimentation rate of up to 3 g C/m$^2$/day (Dahlback and Gunnarson, 1981). Thus, for a farm covering an area of 1 500 m$^2$, the sedimentation of dry matter would amount to about 10 t, and sediment under the rafts would accumulate to about 10 cm per farming season (Sweden, 1983). Data on waste production, sedimentation and sediment accumulation associated with mussel farming are summarized (NCC, 1989) in **Tables 3 and 4**. About 30% of the oyster and mussel farms of France face problems of sedimentation, forcing occasional relocation and abandonment of the beds (Weston, 1991).

26. The deposition of particulate organic wastes can result in physico-chemical changes of the substrate, particularly in the immediate vicinity of the culture site. The enrichment of the sediment with organic material stimulates microbial activity resulting in desoxygenation of the substrate and bottom waters due to reduced interstitial oxygen concentrations and increased oxygen consumption, increased sulphate reduction, increased denitrification, and increased release of inorganic nutrients such as nitrate, nitrite, ammonium, silicate and phosphate from mussel beds (Smaal, 1991). The regeneration of potentially limiting nutrients may increase primary productivity.

27. Benthic communities beneath suspended culture may be affected in various ways (Kaspar *et al.*, 1985). Macrofauna may be lacking entirely in the area directly under the culture site. Around the culture site, species richness is reduced and opportunistic enrichment-tolerant species become predominant. Crabs changed their diet and became abundant as a response to mussel culture in northwest Spain (Freire *et al.*, 1991), where transport of organic material derived from farms was shown to enhance benthic macrofauna biomass beyond the area of the coastal embayment. Based on a literature review, Gowen *et al.* (1988) summarized the possible ecological effects of mussel raft farming (see **Figure 2**).

28. Introductions of bivalves may have negative ecological effects (Chew, 1990), particularly when parasites and diseases are also introduced. The re-introduction of the European flat oyster (*Ostrea edulis*) to Europe from North America resulted in the spread of *Bonamia ostreae*, a blood-cell parasite on oysters, which devastated the European flat oyster industry. Two predators on bivalves, the Japanese oyster drill (*Ceratoderma inornatum* and the oyster flatworm (*Pseudostylochus ostreophagus*) as well as the parasitic copepod *Mytilicola orientalis*, that can greatly affect condition of several bivalve species, were introduced together with the Pacific oyster (*Crassostrea gigas*) from Japan to North America. Also with introductions and transfers of mussel species, there is risk of spreading infectious diseases and parasites that are harmful to mussels and other bivalves (Bower and Figueras, 1989).

### Shrimp culture

29. Most shrimp culture is carried out in earthen ponds, although pens and cages are also used in some cases (Tookwinas, 1990; Walford and Lam, 1987). Shrimp ponds may cover extensive coastal areas which have often required the conversion of rice paddies, salt pans, coconut and sugar plantations, abandoned lands, and mangrove forests (Chong, 1990a; Aitken, 1990).

30. Although there is no doubt that substantial areas of virgin mangrove swamps have been cleared for shrimp pond construction (Terchunian *et al.*, 1986; Kapetsky, 1987a), it is important to recognize that mangrove ecosystems have also been utilized for other purposes, such as

Table 3: Faecal waste production and sedimentation from bivalve farming (from NCC, 1989). References cited in NCC, 1989.

| species and system | faecal production | reference |
|---|---|---|
| *Mytilus galloprovincialis* | 14.3-149.3 mg DW/individual/24h | Arakawa *et al* (1971) |
| *M.edulis* natural shore population | 1.76 gDW/gDW mussel/yr<br>0.13 g C "<br>0.0017 g N "<br>0.00026 g P " | Kautsky and Evans (1987) |
| *M.edulis* rafts | 9.5 kg carbon/m$^2$/yr<br>1.1 kg nitrogen/m$^2$/yr | Rodhouse *et al* (1985) |
| *M.edulis* long-lines | 0.88 kg carbon/m$^2$/yr | Rosenberg and Loo (1983) |
| *M.edulis* rafts | 27 g carbon /m$^2$/24h | Cabanas *et al* (1979) |
| *M.edulis* long-lines | 2.4-3.3 g carbon /m$^2$/24h<br>1.7 (ref.station) | Dahlback and Gunnarsson (1981) |
| M.edulis rafts | 0.5–2.5 g carbon /m$^2$/24h | Tenore *et al* (1982) |

Table 4: Sediment accumulation below bivalve farms (from NCC, 1989). References cited in NCC, 1989.

| species and system | depth | current velocity | sediment accumulation | reference |
|---|---|---|---|---|
| *M.edulis* | 11-13m | "very weak" | 7-30 cm | Weston(1986a) |
| *M.edulis* long lines | 8-13m | ~ 3cm/s | 10-15 cm | Dahlback and Gunnarsson (1981) |
| *M.edulis* | no data | | >1 cm/yr | Misdorp *et al* (1984) |
| *M.edulis* rafts | >15m | up to 200cm/s | no sig. biodeposits mussel shells present | Rodhouse *et al* (1985) |
| M.edulis<br>2 long lines<br>3 raft sites | | "strong currents" | no sig. biodeposits mussel shells present | Earll *et al* (1984) |

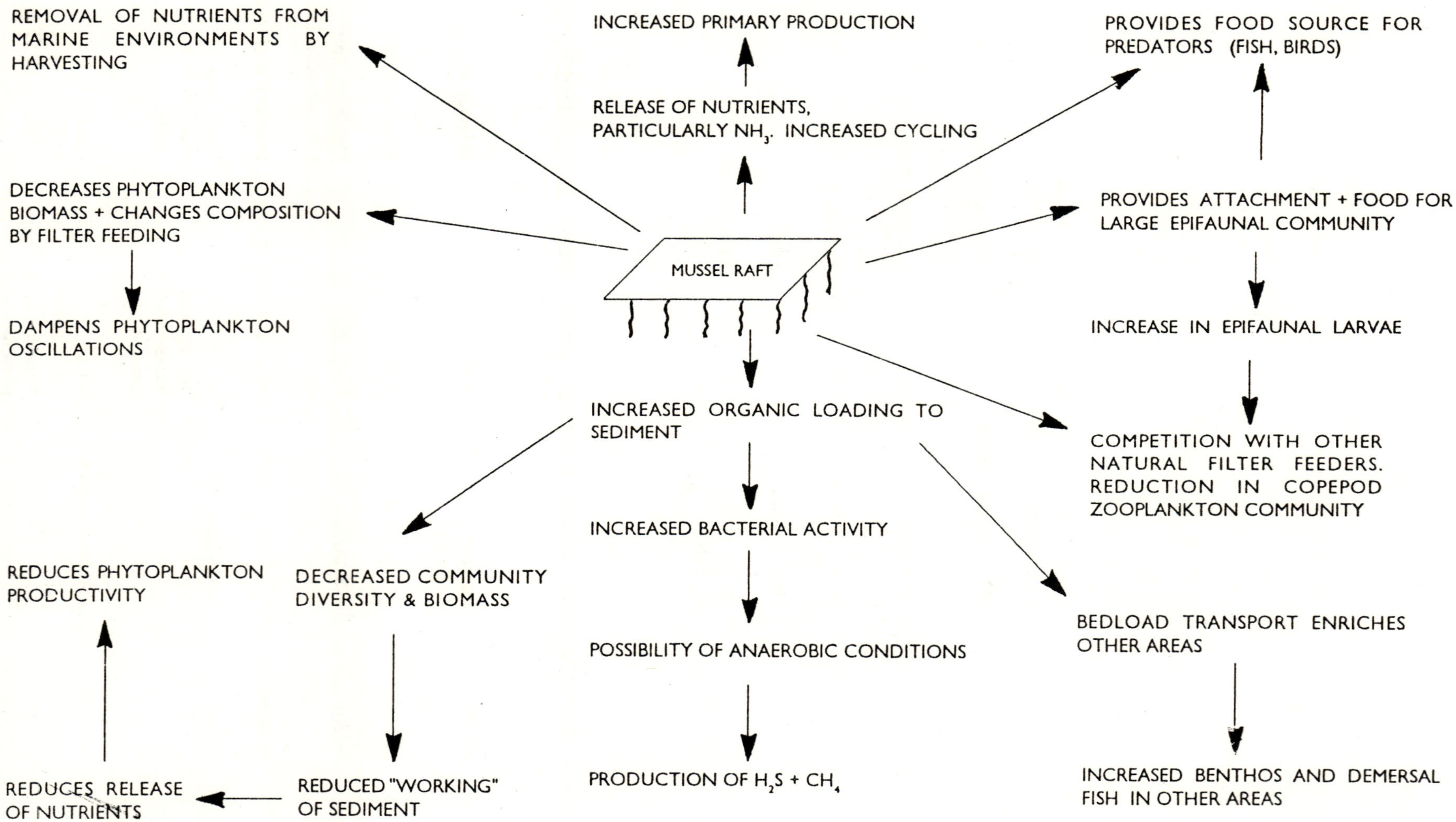


**Figure 2:** Summary of the possible ecological effects of mussel raft farming. Note: some effects are contradictory, and not all effects will be seen at one site (redrawn from Gowen *et al.*,1988)

forestry, agriculture and fishpond culture (Andriawan and Jhamtani, 1989; Soemodihardjo and Soerianegara, 1989; Zamora, 1989; FAO, 1985a; Neal, 1984).

31. Removal of mangroves for pond culture can significantly affect shoreline configuration and coastal erosion patterns, generation and cycling of nutrients in coastal areas as well as habitats of many - also commercially important - species, which use the intertidal ecosystem as breeding, nursery and feeding grounds (Honculada Primavera, 1991; Saclauso, 1989; Matthes and Kapetsky, 1988). Aquatic production patterns may shift from detritus-based to plankton-based food paths, depending on the mangrove area lost and the amount of degradation (Kapetsky, 1987b).

32. Ponds reclaimed from mangrove swamps exhibit typically acid sulphate soils (Pedini, 1981; Simpson and Pedini, 1985, 1987). Oxidation of pyrite ($FeS_2$) occurs during pond-bottom drying which results in the release of sulphuric acid into the pond water and adjacent water bodies causing acidification and the generation of highly toxic soluble aluminium phosphate (Chua *et al.*, 1989) and gill-clogging ferric hydroxide (Singh, 1987). Serious problems of sedimentation and siltation can be expected when mangrove soil in ponds is replaced with soil from upland areas, and dumped into nearby mangrove forests as practised in some projects in Thailand (Chantadisai, 1989). Long-term application of lime to neutralize acid sulphate soils, coupled with fertilization practices, however, may harden pond-bottom soils, rendering them less suitable for shrimp pond culture.

33. Only rather extensive culture methods can be used appropriately in the intertidal mangrove zone, since they rely on tidal flow for supply and exchange of water. Intensive culture methods usually requiring more than 1 m of pondwater depth will also have to allow for pumping for complete drying during pond preparation if located in the intertidal mangrove zone. Poernomo (1990) compares economic and environmental suitability of intertidal and supratidal zones for the various culture systems (see **Figure 3** and **Tables 5 and 6**).

34. Construction of channels for water supply and drainage and pumping of brackishwaters inland results in hydrological changes, siltation and saltwater intrusion (Mahmood, 1987; Cholik and Poernomo, 1987). Pumping and trucking of saltwater to inland backyard hatcheries may affect groundwater quality (Yap, 1990). Abstraction of groundwaters for freshwater supply of intensive pond culture may also result in the salinization of these emptied freshwater aquifers, and certainly had severe consequences of land subsidence in Taiwan (Liao, 1989).

35. It can be expected that the use of fertilizers and feeds (trash fish, mussel meat, shrimp heads and formulated diets) to increase production (Kontara, 1988) will alter water and sediment quality in ponds and adjacent waters. Their excessive use carries the risk of increased nutrient and organic matter loading (Akiyama and Chwang, 1989).

36. Fertilizers, such as triple-superphosphate, urea, cow dung, chicken manure and rice bran (Apud *et al.*, 1983; Chamberlain, 1991; Sin *et al.*, 1989) which are used to promote growth of shrimp food organisms, may contribute to the nutrient and organic load. Use of feeds also generates nutrient and organic loads in form of dissolved metabolites (ammonia, urea and carbon dioxide) and particulate matter (uneaten feeds and faeces), which may result in the build-up of anoxic sediments and over-population of algae in ponds. Up to 30-40% of pond water volume is pumped and drained per day in semi-intensive and intensive pond systems to supply oxygen and to remove excess nutrients and organic matter. Water requirements are, therefore, considerable; for example, 11 000-21 430 $m^3$/t production are required for semi-intensive culture and 29 000-43 000 $m^3$/t for intensive culture in Taiwan (Chien *et al.*, 1988; Wickins, 1986; both cited in Phillips *et al.*, 1991).

37. Effluents discharged will reflect water quality conditions in the pond. Wide ranges have been recorded (Phillips *et al.*, in press) for effluent water quality parameters during a five-month grow-out period at an intensive shrimp farm in Thailand (**Table 7**). A very high organic and nutrient load can be expected in effluents during harvesting, draining and cleaning of ponds, because of the

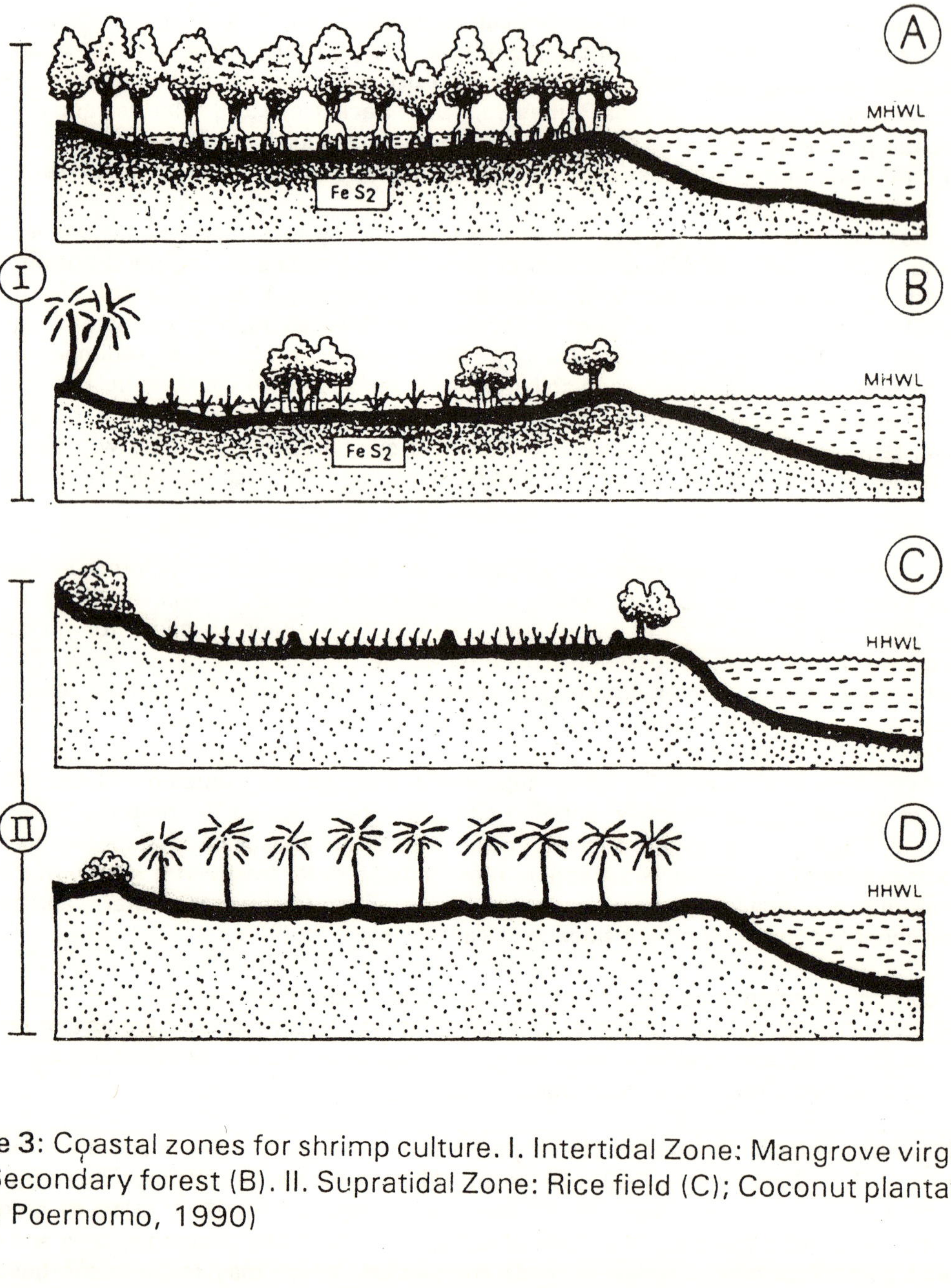


Figure 3: Coastal zones for shrimp culture. I. Intertidal Zone: Mangrove virgin forest (A); Secondary forest (B). II. Supratidal Zone: Rice field (C); Coconut plantation (D). (from Poernomo, 1990)

Table 5: Types of coastal zones for shrimp ponds (from Poernomo, 1990)

| Coastal zone | Tidal range | Soil properties | | Construction work and cost** | Pond productivity | Soil treatment | Application of culture technology |
|---|---|---|---|---|---|---|---|
| | | Type/texture | pH* | | | | |
| INTERTIDAL ZONES | | | | | | | |
| Virgin mangrove forest | Submerged at LHWL | peat/pyrite | 2.5-3.5 | + + + + | Very low initially | Reclamation (drying and leaching) before use | Extensive |
| Secondary mangrove forest (shrub) | Submerge at LHWL | pyrite/peat | 2.4-4.0 | + + + | Very low initially | Reclamation before use | Extensive to semi intensive |
| Grassy swamp | Submerged at MHWL | pyrite/clay loam | 3.5-5.0<br>6.5-7.0 | + + | Low initially | Reclamation before use | Extensive to semi intensive |
| Coconut plantation | Submerged at MHWL along the ditches | pyrite/clay loam | 3.5-5.0<br>6.5-7.0 | + + | Relatively low initially | Reclamation before use | Extensive to semi intensive |
| SUPRATIDAL ZONES | | | | | | | |
| Rice field/dry land crope | Above HHWL | Clay loam to loam | 7.0 | + | High from the beginning | No specific treatment | Intensive only |
| Coconut plantation | Above HHWL | Sandy clay loam | 7.0 | + | High from the beginning | No specific treatment | Intensive only |
| Grass and others | Above HHWL | Sandy loam Loamy Sand | 7.0-8.0 | + | High from the beginning | No specific treatment | Intensive only |
| | | Sandy | 7.0-8.0 | Porous. No good for tambak | – | – | – |

* Soil pH after drying

** + Very easy, least cost
+ + Easy, low cost
+ + + Difficult, high cost
+ + + + Very difficult, very high cost

**Table 6**: Comparison of intertidal and supratidal zones when developed for shrimp tambaks (from Poernomo, 1990)

| Parameters and stage of development | Intertidal zone | Supratidal zone |
|---|---|---|
| Land type | Mangrove and grassy swamps | Irrigated and dry flat land |
| Elevation | Intertidal, between MHWL and MLWL | Above high tide, less than 2m above MHWL |
| Soil type | Mostly potential acid sulphate soils (contains high pyrite and peat to some extent) | Generally does not contain acid sulphate soil |
| Land cost | The undeveloped areas are government owned, can be leased with very low cost | Land is mostly privately owned, or claimed and cultivated, cost high to very high |
| Land clearing | Very costly for forested area | Very minimal |
| Construction coast | Low for extensive ponds with shallow and large sized ponds by very high for intensive ponds | Only for intensive ponds. Low for earthendike ponds, high for concrete dike ponds |
| Development work | Rely mainly on manual labor, mechanisation limited, time consuming | Largely mechanised. Manual only for little finishing work. Construction work can be completed in short time |
| Pre-production pond conditioning | Through reclamation. Several months are required if acid sulphate condition exists | Production operations can be started immediately after construction finished |
| Pond preparation | Pond bottom drying is a chronic problem. Becomes worse if dike quality is not good | Complete drying easy. Time for pond preparation much shorter |
| Pond filling | Through natural gravity during high tide. Minimal pumping in semi-intensive culture | Fully relies on pumps regardless of level of culture technology and stocking density applied |
| Pest control | Difficult to control the entry of noxious extraneous organisms | Much less entry unwanted extraneous organisms, and easier to control if any |
| Harvesting | Time consuming and very much depends on tide condition. It may affect product quality | Fast, can be done any time |
| Environmental impact | Destruction of mangrove swamp environment if not strictly controlled | Landward intrusion of sea water and salination of land and ground water resource |

**Table 7**: The ranges of effluent water quality recorded at an intensive shrimp farm in Thailand during a five-month grow-out period; data from C.K. Lin (from Phillips *et al.*, in press)

| | |
|---|---|
| Pond size (ha) | 0.48 - 0.56 |
| Pond depth (m) | 1.5 - 1.8 |
| Salinity (ppt) | 10 - 35 |
| Temperature (°C) | 22 - 31 |
| pH | 7.5 - 8.9 |
| Total phosphorus (mg/l) | 0.05 - 0.4 |
| Total nitrogen (mg/l) | 0.50 - 3.4 |
| Total ammonia (mg/l) | 0.05 - 0.65 |
| Dissolved oxygen (mg/l) | 4.0 - 7.5 |
| Chlorophyll a (μg/l) | 20 - 250 |
| Total suspended solids (mg/l) | 30 - 190 |
| Water exchange frequency (%/day) | 5 - 40 |

additional discharge of material previously bound to sediment particulate matter. Unfortunately, there is a general lack of field-data specific to the amount and quality of effluent loadings from shrimp ponds as well as to related ecological effects on receiving waterbodies. However, the potentially adverse effects of the discharge of effluents rich in nutrients and organic material may include increased sedimentation and siltation, hypoxia, hypernutrification, and alterations of productivity and community structures of benthic communities.

38. A variety of chemicals is used in shrimp aquaculture (Sunaryanto, 1988; Baticados *et al.*, 1990; Liu, 1989). Antibiotics such as chloramphenicol, oxytetracycline, furazolidone, streptomycin, nitrofurazone, are applied in shrimp hatcheries and grow-out ponds to treat and to prevent outbreaks of disease. Over-use of antibiotics (Brown, 1989) could be very dangerous due to the potential generation of drug-resistant shrimp pathogens (e.g., *Vibrio*) and the risk of transfer of drug resistance to human pathogens. Spread of drug-resistant strains is probable in shrimp culture areas with a high concentration of farms. Abuse of antibiotics in Taiwanese hatcheries resulted in poor resistance and survival of shrimp under grow-out conditions (Lin, 1989). Abuse of formalin and malachite green is known to be harmful to algae and zooplankton, including penaeid nauplii. Unwanted species are being eradicated by applying copper sulphate as algicide, plant-based biodegradable piscicides, such as tobacco dust (nicotine), tea seed cake (saponin), derris root extract (rotenone); as well as organo-pesticides as molluscicides, such as chlorinated hydrocarbons (DDT, endrin, aldrin, thiodan) and organotins (brestan and aquatin). These organo-pesticides are of particular concern due to their toxicity and persistence, and their potential implications for product quality and human health. No ecological effect has so far been reported for disinfectants and chemicals for water and soil treatment such as with sodium hypochlorite, benzalkonium chloride, calcium carbide, Na-EDTA, and zeolites.

39. There is growing evidence that some shrimp pathogens such as the infectious hypodermal haematopoietic necrosis virus (IHHNV) and monodonbacilovirus (MBV) have been disseminated through introduction and transfer of commercial shrimp species. Outbreaks of shrimp disease have been also attributed to excessive intensification and deterioration of water and sediment quality in shrimp ponds and adjacent waters due to waste overloading. Soft-shell syndrome, red disease and blue shrimps appear to be linked to the acid-sulphate soil problem (Baticados *et al.*, 1990; Brock, 1991), although conclusive evidence is still lacking. Due to disease and pond management problems, resulting in production losses, farms have been abandoned and relocated. In this connection, Lin (1989) has summarized the causes for the collapse in 1988 of the shrimp industry in Taiwan (see **Annex 1**).

40. A further biological implication of shrimp culture refers to the required seed and feed inputs. Even though stocking of hatchery-reared postlarvae is increasing, wild-caught postlarvae are often preferred (Hirono and Van Eys, 1990), which may lead to overfishing of postlarvae, and, to the discarding of an estimated 10 kg of larvae and fry of other species for 1 kg of shrimp larvae harvested (Silas, 1987).

41. In 1988, shrimp farming in Asia absorbed 180 000 t of fish meal which is used for compound feeds; and about 1.1 million t of shrimp feed may be needed by the year 2000. This increasing demand may eventually encroach on species caught for human food as well as on juveniles of these species (New and Wijkstrom, 1990).

Finfish culture

42. Most coastal finfish culture is carried out in ponds, pens, cages, tanks and raceways (Chua, 1982; Padlan, 1982; Beveridge, 1987).

43. Extensive land degradation, especially of mangrove areas, has been experienced with the farming of herbivorous and detritus-feeding fish species such as milkfish and mullets in brackishwater ponds even before shrimp culture started to expand. Brackishwater milkfish/mullet culture also faces potential ecological problems related to acid-sulphate soils, deterioration of water

and sediment quality, overfertilization and chemical usage (organotins as molluscicides), which may severely affect adjacent mangrove ecosystems (Poernomo and Singh, 1982; Ti *et al.*, 1982; Kapetsky, 1982).

44. However, potential ecological problems related to nutrient and organic enrichment within and outside the culture unit are more likely to be found with semi-intensive and, in particular, with intensive farming of carnivorous fishes where provision of feeds is required (Mok, 1982). Nutrient and organic wastes, in dissolved and particulate forms, stemming from uneaten food and excreta, are generally characterized by an increase in suspended solids (SS), biochemical oxygen demand (BOD), chemical oxygen demand (COD), and content of carbon, nitrogen and phosphorus. Unfortunately, most of the available information on wastes released from fishfarms relates to temperate species.

45. The following are examples of effluent loads from land-based fishfarms. The yearly oxygen demand and nutrient release per ton of rainbow trout produced at a Danish pond farm was reported to be 300 kg $BOD_6$/t/y, and 10 kg Total-P/t/y and 81 kg Total-N/t/y (Sweden, 1983). For tanks stocked with adult Atlantic salmon, a range of values was found (Bergheim and Forsberg, 1992) for effluent loadings expressed as g/kg fish/24 hours : 0.5-1.4 g suspended dry matter (SDM), 0.01-0.05 g total phosphorus (TP), 0.15-0.30 total nitrogen (TN) and 0.1-0.2 g total ammonia nitrogen (TAN), with a food conversion ratio of 1.0-1.2 dry feed per kilogramme fish weight gain. The results of this study are shown in **Figure 4**, where effluent loading is related to the amount of food given.

46. Rosenthal *et al.* (1988) found wide differences when summarizing estimated loads from various intensive trout farms using pond and tank systems (**Table 8**). More recent comparative analysis (Beveridge *et al.*, 1991) on effluent quality in freshwater salmonid aquaculture (**Table 9**) confirms the variability of data for effluent loadings. It is concluded that there are many variables governing effluent quality, including species, size, method and intensity of culture, management, temperature, mode of discharge and the extent of dilution or treatment prior to discharge.

47. Regarding the release of wastes from marine cage farms, estimates of solid waste production from salmonid farms range from 0.3 to 0.7 dry weight of waste feed and faeces per kilogramme of fish produced (Weston, 1991). A typical Norwegian net pen farm with an annual salmon production of 200 t and well-controlled feeding techniques is said to provide an annual loading level of 2 t of phosphorus, 18 t nitrogen and 100 t oxygen consumption as $BOD_7$ (Seymour and Bergheim, 1991). Gowen and Bradbury (1987) predicted the generation of 19.4 t of organic carbon waste, 2.2 t of organic nitrogen waste and 4.0 t of soluble nitrogenous waste from a salmonid farm with an annual production of 50 t using 100 t of food per year (see **Figures 5 and 6**). Results from a field study indicated that up to 76% of the carbon and 76% of the nitrogen fed to cage-farmed salmon is released into the marine environment as solid and soluble waste, and, that the main factors controlling the level of enrichment of the benthos and water column are the size of the farm, husbandry and the hydrography at the site (Gowen *et al.*, 1988).

48. It is evident that considerable water exchange rates are required for waste removal and oxygen supply in both land-based and sea-based fishfarms. The dilution/dispersal, areal distribution and sedimentation of the released waste and its potential ecological effects around fishfarms are determined by current velocities and depth of waterbodies receiving the waste load from pond/tank effluents and cages.

49. It has been argued that the discharge from fishfarms of dissolved inorganic nitrogen (ammonium, nitrate and nitrite), and, in the case of brackishwater environments, phosphorus, may affect the standing stock, species composition, or productivity of phytoplankton and macroalgae. Weston (1991), however, anticipated localized and measurable effects on microalgal communities only in cases of unusually dense culture activity in poorly flushed coastal embayments (see also Aure and Stigebrandt, 1990; Frid and Mercer, 1989; Turrel and Munro, 1989).

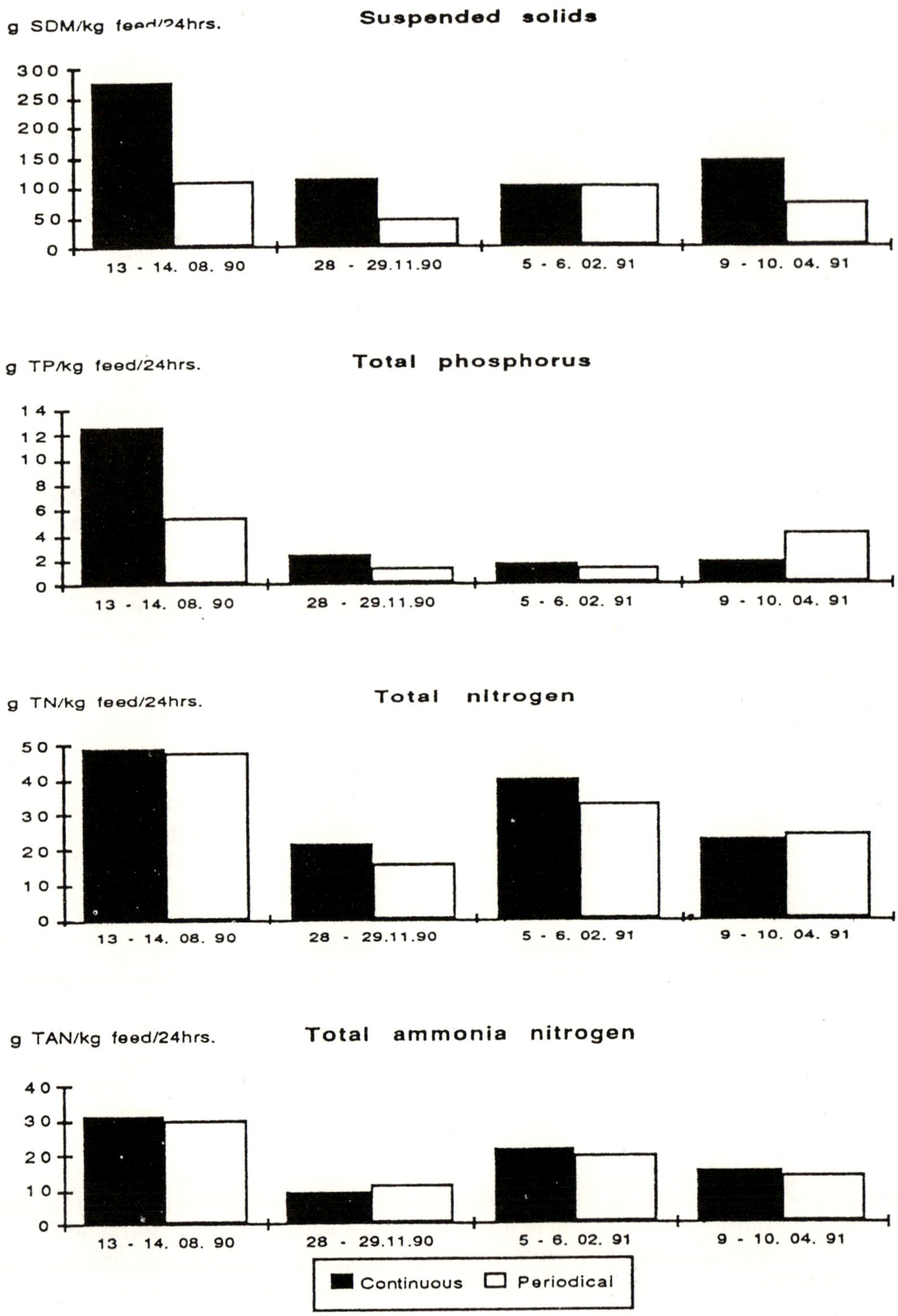


Daily effluent loadings from tanks stocked with adult Atlantic salmon at two different feeding regimes. Unit : g/kg feed /24 hrs.
Continuous feeding. : feeding supply 24 hrs./day
Periodical feeding : feeding supply 4 - 6 hrs./day

**Figure 4:** Example of effluent loadings from tanks stocked with adult Atlantic salmon (from Bergheim and Forsberg, 1992)

**Table 8**: Estimated loads from various intensive trout farms using pond and tank systems (from Rosenthal *et al.,* 1988). References cited in Rosenthal *et al.*, 1988.

| System | Species | Size | Feeding rate (%) bodyweight | Feed type | Net loading | Reference |
|---|---|---|---|---|---|---|
| Tanks and ponds | Brown trout (biomass 2260 kg) | 2.2-100 g | 17.5-1.3% | dry pellets manual + automatic | 11.5 g COD/kg fish/24h<br>2.7 g $BOD_7$/kg fish/24h<br>0.05 g Total-P/kg fish/24h<br>0.9 g SS/kg fish/24h | Bergheim *et al.* (1982) |
| Tanks and ponds | Brown trout (biomass 7320 kg) | 1.0-25.0 g + brood stock | 3-6% | dry + wet pellets, manual | 75.3 g COD/kg/24h<br>83.3 g $BOD_7$/kg/24h<br>0.43 g Total-P/kg/24h<br>0.24 g $PO_4$-P/kg/24h<br>1.4-3.8 g Total-N/kg/24h | Bergheim *et al.* (1982) |
| Ponds | Brown trout, rainbow trout (biomass 2690 kg) | 0.2-500 g | 0.55-4.5% | dry pellets manual | 17.0 g COD/kg/24h<br>7.1 g SS/kg/24h<br>0.45 g Total-N/kg/24h<br>0.08 g Total-P/kg/24h<br>0.05 g $PO_4$-P/kg/24h | Bergheim *et al.* (1982) |
| Tanks and ponds | Brown trout (biomass 5970 kg) | 1-550 g | 0.5-16% | dry, automatic | 3.1 g COD/kg/24h<br>1.6 g $BOD_7$/kg/24h<br>1.2 g SS/kg/24h<br>0.13 g Total-N/kg/24h<br>0.05 g Total-P/kg/24h<br>0.03 g $PO_4$-P/kg/24h | Bergheim *et al.* (1982) |
| Ponds 12 700m$^2$ | Rainbow trout | 35-150 g<br>500-2000 g | ? | dry pellets | 0.4-0.8 g Total-N/kg/24h<br>0.05 g Total-P/kg/24h<br>1.6-4.6 g $BOD_7$/kg/24h | Bergheim + Selmer- Olsen (1978) |
| Ponds | Rainbow trout | 2.0-300 g | ? | dry pellets, wet feed | 0.5-1.4 g Total-N/kg/24h<br>0.13-0.18 h Total-P/kg/24h<br>1.9-5.7 g $BOD_5$/kg/24h | Markham (1978) |

**Table 9**: Loadings of suspended solids (SS), nutrients and biochemical oxygen demand (BOD) from freshwater salmonid culture (from Beveridge *et al.*, 1991). References cited in Beveridge *et al.*, 1991.

| SS | BOD | $NH_4$-N | $NO_2$-N | $NO_3$-N | Total N | $PO_4$ | Total P | Ref. |
|---|---|---|---|---|---|---|---|---|
| (a) g kg fish$^{-1}$ day$^{-1}$ | | | | | | | | |
| 0.0-7.1 | 1.6-2.7 | - | - | - | 0.1-3.8 | 0.02-0.27 | 0.01-0.43 | a |
| - | 1.4-8.1 | - | - | - | - | - | - | c |
| 0.8-0.9 | - | 0.3-0.8 | - | 0.13-0.21 | - | 0.07-0.17 | - | b |
| - | - | 0.03 | - | 0.05 | 0.12 | 0.033 | 0.10 | d |
| (b) kg ton fish$^{-1}$ annum$^{-1}$ | | | | | | | | |
| 474-4015 | 510-990 | 37-180 | - | 0-548 | - | - | 22-110 | e |
| 1350 | 285 | 55.5 | 1.81 | 10.2 | - | - | 15.7 | f |
| | 350 | 45 | - | - | 83 | - | 11 | g |
| (c) g kg feed$^{-1}$ | | | | | | | | |
| - | 80-300 | - | - | - | - | - | - | c |
| 183 | 165 | 25 | 0.27 | 0 | - | 26 | 4.0 | h |
| 80-280 | 100-370 | - | - | - | 37-48 | - | 4.7-10.8 | i |

[a]Bergheim et al. (1982); [b]Clark et al. (1985); [c]Butz and Vens Cappell (1982); [d]Korzeniewski et al. (1982); [e]Alabaster (1982); [f]Solbe (1982); [g]Warrer-Hansen (1982); [h]Butz (1988); [i]Makinen (1988).

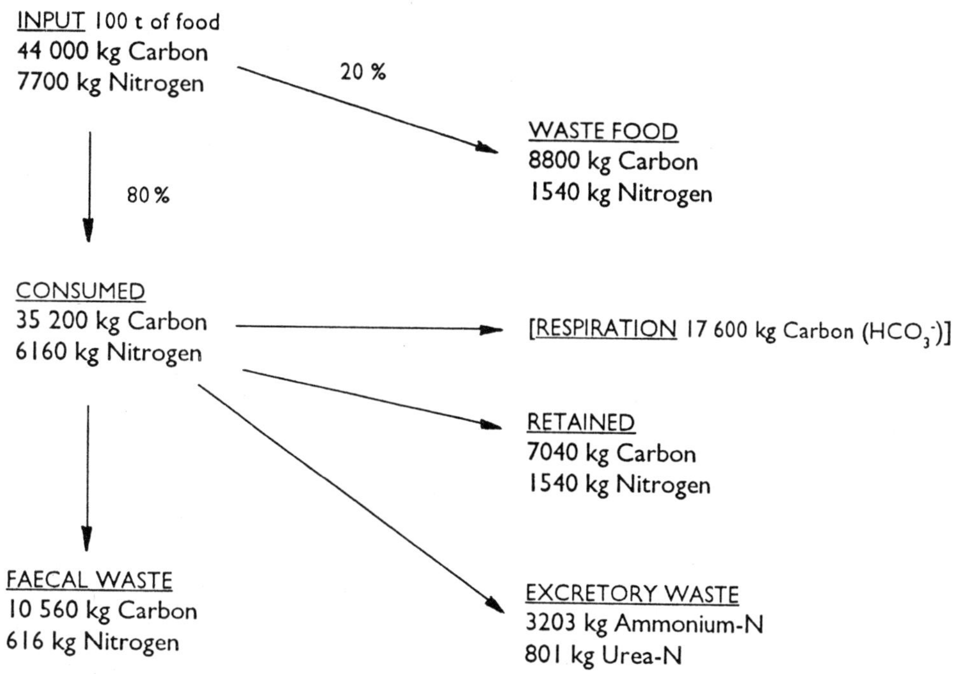


**Figure 5:** The estimated flux of carbon and nitrogen through a salmonid farm with an annual production of 50 t (from Gowen and Bradbury, 1987).

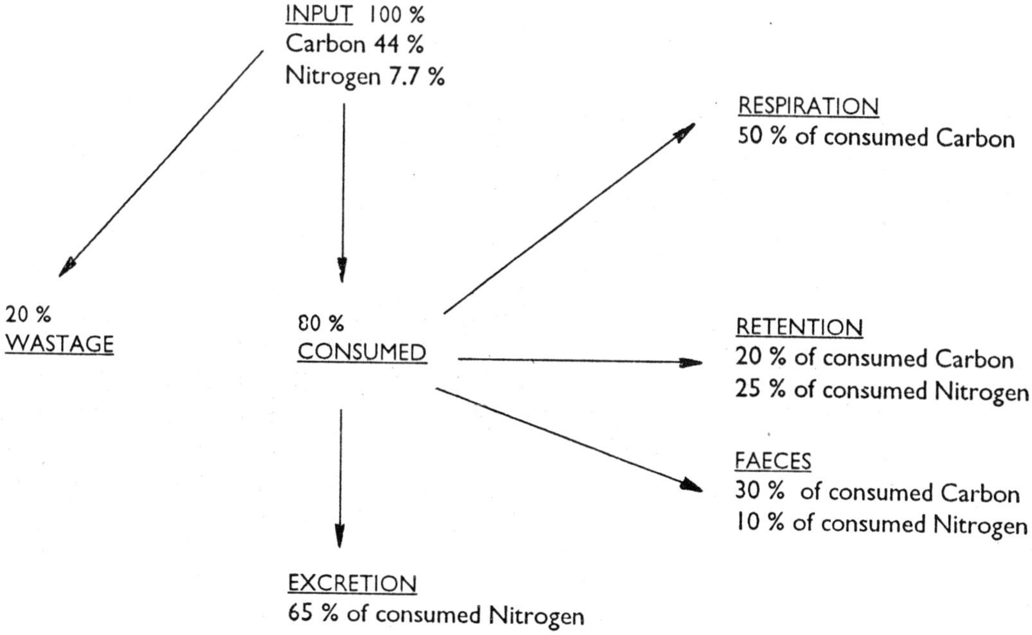


**Figure 6:** The estimated average flux of carbon and nitrogen thrcugh a salmonid farm (from Gowen and Bradbury, 1987)

50. The particulate organic matter released settles in the vicinity of the farm if the settling velocity of the particles is higher than the water current velocity. The solids falling to the seabed are enriched in carbon, nitrogen and phosphorus relative to the natural sediments (Holmer, 1991), possibly causing physico-chemical changes in sediments below or adjacent to fishfarming operations, including increase in organic carbon content, followed by increased sediment oxygen consumption rates and decreased sediment redox potentials (Brown *et al.*, 1987), generation of hydrogen sulphide and methane (Lumb, 1989), and increases in inorganic and organic nitrogen (Kaspar *et al.*, 1988), phosphorus, silicon, calcium, copper and zinc (Rosenthal *et al.*, 1988). However, these physical and chemical effects have been reported to be limited only to the immediate vicinity of fish farms.

51. The areal extent of ensuing ecological effects on macrobenthic communities underneath and around cage culture can be described (NCC, 1989) according to the following patterns (see also **Table 10**) : (a) lack of macrobenthos (the azoic zone, if present at all, usually only below cages), (b) dominance of enrichment-tolerant species (the opportunistic zone, covering an area of up to 30 m from the site) and (c) a gradual return to background conditions, normally occurring within 30 m of the farm, although effects may extend occasionally to up to 100 m off the farm site. Similar effects on the benthic community in the vicinity of discharge pipes from land-based fish farms can be expected, although no specific field-data were available.

52. Magnitude and areal extent of enrichment effects will generally depend on a variety of factors such as farm production characteristics, depth, bottom topography, current velocity and exposure to increased water movements (e.g., storms) which will determine the lateral spread of settling particles, organic input per unit area, and scouring and redistribution of bottom wastes (see also Hakanson *et al.*, 1988; Lauren-Maatta *et al.*, 1991; Kupka Hansen *et al.*, 1991). The ability of the indigenous communities to assimilate and mineralize organic wastes may also be important.

53. A wide range of chemicals is used in finfish culture. These include therapeutants and biocides, vaccines, hormones, vitamins, flesh pigments, anaesthetics, disinfectants, water treatment compounds and chemicals present in materials used in the fabrication of aquaculture units. The use of chemicals varies greatly with species, intensity of culture and location. **Table 11** indicates the diversity of methods and purposes of chemical applications. The amount used and mode of application will determine the extent of the ecological effects.

54. With regard to antibiotics (Grave *et al.*, 1990), which are usually administered in feed, there is evidence that only 20-30% are actually ingested by the fish; thus, approximately 70-80% reaches the environment (Samuelsen, 1989), notably from uneaten medicated food. Oxytetracycline, for example, may be deposited in sediments, where it may remain in concentrations capable of causing antibacterial effects for 12 weeks after cessation of treatment (Jacobsen and Berglind, 1988). Antibiotics may spread to the present benthic fauna or to the wild fish by direct feeding on farm wastes. Antibiotic resistant strains may develop in aerobic and facultative anaerobic bacteria groups, which may affect rates and patterns of bacterial mineralization and decomposition in sediments (Holmer, 1991; Bjorklund *et al.*, 1990).

55. The use of the organophosphorus compounds trichlorfon (Neguvon) and dichlorvos (Nuvan) for treatment of salmon lice has caused concern because of their potential toxicity to non-target organisms such as lobsters, crabs and mussels (Egidius and Moster, 1987), and larvae of herring and lobster (McHenery *et al.*, 1991). However, predictions of assumed toxic effects still require data on inputs, chemical behaviour, degradation, persistence and distribution of the toxicant.

56. Antifoulants, such as tributyltin (TBT), which have been widely used to treat submerged structures and nets in cage and pen culture, are now much less commonly used as fears about the accumulation of organotin- and copper-based compounds in farmed fish flesh have grown (Beveridge *et al.*, 1991).

57. The consequences of introductions and transfers of marine fish may be widespread and

**Table 10**: A summary of studies of the effects of marine cage culture on the macrobenthos (from NCC, 1989). References cited in NCC, 1989.

| Species and system | Effects | Reference |
|---|---|---|
| Coho salmon cages, Puget Sound | High abundance and low diversity directly below cages, dominated by *Capitella capitata* | Pease (1977) |
| Yellowtail, Uchiura Bay, Japan | Increase in opportunistic polychaetes and decrease in relative proportion of molluscs and crustaceans with increased organic inputs | Kitamori (1977) |
| Atlantic salmon cages, Ireland | Azoic below cages, zone around cages dominated by *Capitella capitata* | Stewart (1984) |
| Atlantic salmon cages, Norway | Three farms examined:<br>1. low diversity and community dominated by opportunistic species.<br>2. biostimulated below cages<br>3. "minimal" effect below cages | Ervik *et al.* (1985) |
| Atlantic salmon cages, Scotland | Azoic zone below some farms | Earll *et al.* (1984) |
| Atlantic salmon cages, Shetland | Azoic zones below some farms. Zones below and outside cages dominated by *Capitella capitata*. Effects restricted to 40m of cages | Dixon (1986) |
| Atlantic salmon cages, Scotland | Azoic zone below cages, surrounded by *C. capitata* and *Scolelepis fuliginosa* out to 8m from the site. [enriched zone up to 25m and clean from>25m] | Brown *et al.* (1987) |

**Table 11**: Chemicals used in aquaculture. FW = Freshwater; SW = Saltwater. Application methods: B = Bath; A = Addition to the system; F = Flush; D = Dip; I = Injection; S = Spray; T = Treated food (from NCC, 1989).

| CHEMICAL | USE | FW/SW | METHOD | REMARKS |
|---|---|---|---|---|
| THERAPEUTANTS | | | | |
| Acetic acid | ectoparasites | FW | D | Use with Cu $SO_4$ in hard water areas |
| Formalin | ectoparasites | FW/SW | D A | 165-250 ppm up to 1 hour, 20 ppm 4 hours use in sea cages as bath – common |
| Malachite Green | ectoparasites and fungus | FW/SW | D F S B | Eggs and fish, 100 ppm 30 sec. 4 ppm 1 hour common in fw, occasional use in cages as a dye marker |
| Acriflavin (or Proflavine hemisulphate) | ectoparasites fungus and bacteria | FW | D | Mostly for surface bacteria, fish and eggs occasional use only |
| Nuvan (dichlorvos) | salmon lice | SW | B | 1ppm for 1 hour, canvas round sea cage |
| Salt | ectoparasites | FW | D B | Occasional alternative to formalin |
| Buffered Iodine | Bacteriocide | FW | B | Use to disinfect eggs 10 mins 1000 ppm |
| Oxytetracycline | Bacteriocide | FW/SW | T | Antibiotic widely used for systemic disease |
| Oxolinic acid | Bacteriocide | FW/SW | T | Antibiotic widely used for systemic disease |
| Romet 30 (Sulfadimethoxine and orthomeprim) | Bacteriocide | FW/SW | T | Antibiotic for systemic disease |
| Tribrissen (Trimethoprim/ sulphadiazine) | Bacteriocide | FW/SW | T | Third most widely used antibiotic |
| Hayamine 3500 | Surfactant/ Bacteriocide | FW | A | Quaternary ammonium compound used for treating bacterial gill diseases |
| Benzalkonium Chloride | Bacteriocide | FW | A | Surface antibacterial; 'Roccel' (similar to above) |
| Chloramine T | Bacteriocide | FW | A | As above, also effective for some protozoa |
| VACCINES | | | | |
| Vibrio Anguillarum vaccine | | SW | B | Not widely used |
| Enteric Redmouth vaccine | | FW | B S I | Widely used in trout culture |
| Aeromonas Salmonicida Vibro Anguillarum vaccine | | SW | I | Not widely used |
| ANAESTHETICS | | | | |
| MS222 (tricaine methane-sulfonate) | | FW/SW | B | Widely used approx 1:10,000 dilution |
| Benzocane | | FW/SW | B | Widely used, requires acetone to dissolve |
| Carbon dioxide | | FW/SW | B | Sometimes used at harvest |
| DISINFECTANTS | | | | |
| Calcium hypochlorite | | FW/SW | S | General disinfectant for tanks etc. |
| liquid Iodophore e.g. FAM 30 | | FW/SW | S | For equipment and footbaths |
| sodium hydroxide | | FW | S | Most commonly used for earth ponds |
| WATER TREATMENT | | | | |
| Lime | | FW | A | Used in earth ponds |
| Potassium permanganate | | FW/SW | B A | Oxidizer and detoxifier |
| Copper sulphate | | FW/SW | A | Algicide and herbicide |

irreversible. Primary concerns with the introduction of Pacific salmon species (*Oncorhynchus kisutch, O. gorbuscha* and *O. keta*) into Atlantic waters have been on the possible competition with Atlantic salmon (*Salmo salar*) in spawning streams and nursery areas, as well as on importation of diseases such as infectious haemapoietic necrosis (IHN) caused by a virus, and bacterial kidney disease (BKD) caused by *Renibacterium salmoninarum* (Sindermann, 1986). By 1987, Atlantic salmon in about 30 Norwegian rivers had been infested by *Gyrodactylus salaris*, an ectoparasitic trematode, which found its way to Norway via salmon smolts imported from Sweden in the mid-1970s (Folke and Kautsky, 1989). The introduction of "Tilapia mossambica" (*Oreochromis mossambicus*) is considered a "real nightmare" (Juliano *et al.*, 1989) for Philippine brackishwater farming, due to competition for food with farmed milkfish.

58. In a general review, Baltz (1991) concludes that more than 120 species of marine and euryhaline fishes have been successfully introduced around the world. Most introductions either did not establish populations, did not achieve their objectives if introduced deliberately, or often had deleterious effects if the species became established. Biodiversity of coastal ecosystems may be threatened due to extinction of native species and disruption of structure and function in natural communities. The extent of genetic interactions between cultured and wild populations will depend principally on the probability of breeding between strains, races or species (e.g., extent of escapes, ecological or behavioural barriers to "interbreeding") and the relative size of the breeding population of escaped fish in comparison to the wild breeding population.

59. An increase of abundance, biomass and diversity of fish and other species in the vicinity of fish culture structures, in particular cages and pens, can be expected as the culture site is likely to represent an area of increased food availability (uneaten food, dense macrobenthic populations) for wild fish communities.

60. Farming of carnivorous fish relies on fishmeal-based feed inputs, and it has been estimated that 5.3 t of fish is required to support 1 t of harvested cage-farmed salmon (Folke and Kautsky, 1989; Folke, 1988). With increasing demand for fishmeal-based feeds, aquaculture may in certain cases indirectly interact with natural fish populations.

Negative feedback effects

61. It is important to recognize that it is often aquaculture itself which is affected by ecological changes deriving from farming practices. For example, water currents may be reduced significantly due to farm structures (cages, pens, rafts, etc.), which may lead to increased deposition and accumulation of organic wastes underneath or around the farming unit, increase in siltation and water quality deterioration (e.g., increase in turbidity due to high content of suspended matter). In addition, oxygen supply may be reduced, and outgassing of hydrogen sulphide and methane from bottom sediments may occur which will further affect growth performance and increase susceptibility to disease (Lumb, 1989).

62. Pond culture which relies on tidal flow or pumping for water exchange may also face a steady increase of water quality deterioration. For example, total water exchange requirements of Indonesian intensive shrimp pond systems will often exceed the flow rate of the tidal creek that serves as the supply canal and drainage ditch. The net result is that instead of replacing waste with clean water, these farms are very often recycling waste water (Chamberlain, 1991). Extensive culture systems relying on the natural productivity of waters used may reduce or deviate water flow through farming structures and heavy siltation, thereby reducing the availability of food and nutrients.

63. Chemicals used may also present a potential risk to cultured organisms (Ackefors *et al.*, 1990), and may result in contamination of aquaculture products which reduces product quality and consumer acceptance. The development of drug-resistant pathogens, resident (and possibly dormant) both within and around the farming unit, may have serious negative feedback effects on farm productivity. The over-use of chemicals in hatcheries may result in reduced fitness, poor

growth and decreased survival rates during the grow-out phase. Pond soils may be rendered less suitable by excessive chemical treatment.

64. Predators such as fish and birds are attracted to the cultured as well as natural population of fish in the area and the ready supply of fish feed. There is the possibility not only that these predators damage and consume valuable fish, but also enhance disease in the area by serving as intermediate hosts in the life cycle of parasites. Predators as well as grazers on the epiphyton of farm structures can also damage netting or other enclosure material, resulting in escapes.

65. The magnitude of negative ecological feedback effects of coastal aquaculture practices may increase with expansion and/or intensification. An increase in the acreage and/or number of farming units (ponds, racks, rafts, cages, etc.) and farms may be followed by deterioration of required environmental quality within and beyond the aquaculture area.

66. As a result of expansion of farming systems relying on naturally available food and nutrients, the natural productivity of waterbodies in coastal areas may be exhausted. Large-scale coverage and degradation of tidal habitats, including mangrove areas, may also affect wild seed supply. Clearly, aggregations of farms will exhibit cumulative effects of waste release and increased oxygen demand. Negative feedback effects of siltation, turbidity, build-up of organic-rich sediments, hypoxic or anoxic bottom waters, toxic outgassing, spread of diseases, etc., may then affect all farms in the area, particularly when located in sheltered and shallow coastal embayments with low water exchange rates. Land-based farming systems have faced similar problems, such as, for example, intensive shrimp culture in Taiwan and Thailand where farms tend to cluster on suitable sites which resulted in very serious self-pollution problems (Csavas, in press). Csavas states that "drained water of one farm is often re-used by its neighbours, making thus water exchange in the heavily stocked ponds a futile exercise"

### III.3 Degradation of Coastal Environments and Potential Effects on Coastal Aquaculture

67. The coastal zone as an economic entity provides sites for a wide range of activities, such as agriculture (e.g., rice, coco palm, bananas), forestry (e.g., mangrove, nypa palm), fisheries and aquaculture, human settlements, manufacturing and extractive industries (e.g., sand mining, oil, minerals), waste disposal, ports and marine transportation, land transportation infrastructure, water control and supply projects, shore protection works, tourism and recreation. The multiple resource uses or activities in coastal areas may produce a variety of changes in environmental or socio-economic conditions, which in turn may result in an impact of social concern. **Annex 2** gives an overview on issues of potential impact resulting from multiple uses of coastal resources. **Figure 7** illustrates various sources of pollution within the coastal zone. Readers further interested in aspects of coastal and marine pollution are referred to : Phillips and Tanabe (1989); Gomez *et al.* (1990); Sen Gupta *et al.* (1990); GESAMP (1990b); UNEP (1990b); GESAMP (1990a); GESAMP (1987); GESAMP (1980); Maclean (1989).

68. It is important to recognize that in many coastal areas, pollution and habitat modification stemming from human activities other than aquaculture are increasingly affecting resource use productivity of aquaculture as well as limiting success and development possibilities of the aquaculture industry (Stickney, 1990; Chua and Tech, 1990; Menasveta, 1987).

69. The following are examples of potential pollution threats to coastal aquaculture (Chua *et al.*, 1989). High organic and microbial loading in sewage discharged from densely populated urban and resort areas can contaminate cultured shellfish thereby rendering this aquaculture produce unsuitable for humans, particularly if consumed raw or partially cooked. As an example, coliform counts in excess of 1 000/100 ml have been recorded in Manila Bay, which is one of the major oyster and mussel culture sites in the Philippines. In 1979, an outbreak of gastro-enteritis was experienced in Singapore, which was traced to oyster meat imported from the Philippines. As a result of this incident, seafood demand from the Philippines declined. Heavy organic pollution due

a. Oil slicks and domestic wastes from ports
b. Domestic wastes from urban settlement
c. Heavy metals, chemicals from industrial sites
d. Solid and domestic wastes from beach resorts
e. High suspended solids from sand mining
f. Nutrients and organic matter load from shrimp farms
g. Pesticides and nutrients from agriculture
h. Alteration of coastal hydrologic regime caused by freshwater discharge from reservoir
i. Pesticides, nutrients and organic matter load from fish farms
j. High organic wastes and drugs from piggery
k. High suspended solids in mollusk farms
l. High suspended solids and nutrients from cage farms

**Figure 7:** Various sources of pollution within the coastal zone (from Chua *et al.*, 1989)

to effluents from Malaysian piggeries and Thai sugar mills, characterized by high biochemical oxygen demand, seriously damaged cockle beds and other cultured organisms. Thai shrimp and oyster farms were severely affected by liquid waste from a distillery.

70. Heavy metals found in industrial effluents may be found in the animals cultured in the receiving waters. In Jakarta Bay (Indonesia), the analysis of fish and shellfish samples showed that WHO standards for heavy metals were exceeded in 76% of the samples tested for cadmium; 51% for copper; 44% for lead; 38% for mercury; and 2% for chromium. Serious oil spills can cause large-scale fish kills, and obvious effects on aquaculture include the contamination of farming structures and tainting of farmed organisms.

71. High levels of pesticides, stemming from agricultural run-off, can be lethal to cultured organisms, while lower doses are believed to produce sublethal effects such as pathological changes in various organs.

72. The release of inorganic and organic nutrients into marine ecosystems can cause hypernutrification, and possibly phytoplankton blooms. Cultured fish can be killed by algal blooms through sudden water quality deterioration (suffocation due to gill damage and/or oxygen depletion) after collapse and decomposition of a bloom. In particular, bivalve culture is facing serious problems associated with the increasing occurrence of toxic phytoplankton blooms caused by a relatively small number of algal species producing a range of toxins, the effects of which include mortality of cultured stocks, as well as human illness and even death after consumption of contaminated bivalves (Shumway, 1990, 1989).

### III.4 Social Implications of Coastal Aquaculture Developments

73. The environmental impacts of and on coastal aquaculture may have serious adverse socio-economic and human health implications (Huss, 1991; Bernoth, 1991a).

74. There is concern that large-scale mangrove conversion for shrimp and fish farming in Latin American and Asian countries has affected rural communities which traditionally depended on mangrove resources for their livelihood (Chua, in press; Mena Millar, 1989; Nath Roy, 1984). According to Bailey (1988), "the expansion of shrimp mariculture into mangrove habitat generally involves the transformation of a multi-use/multi-user coastal resource into a privately owned single-purpose resource. Moreover, the costs of coastal ecosystem disruption for society may include coastal erosion, saltwater intrusion into groundwater and agricultural fields, and a reduction in supply of a wide range of valuable goods and services produced from the resources available in mangrove forests or other coastal wetlands."

75. Likewise, Smith and Pestano-Smith (1985) stated that large-scale aquaculture enterprises frequently displace small-scale fishermen and aquaculturists. Unfortunately, competition for land and water resources also results in use conflicts (Shang, 1990; Stansell, 1992), sometimes with ensuing violence, as seen between rice and shrimp farmers in Thailand (New, 1991).

76. Several economic disasters due to significant aquaculture production losses have been attributed to self-pollution as well as to increasing coastal water pollution which fueled disease outbreaks and harmful phytoplankton blooms (Rosenberry, 1990; Chua, in press; New, 1990a; Okaichi, 1991; Maclean, 1991).

77. Consumption of raw and partially cooked shellfish grown in coastal waters receiving high organic and microbial loadings from urban sewage effluents can result in severe consequences for human health, including gastro-intestinal disorders, gastro-enteritis, infectious hepatitis, cholera and typhoid fever (Shuval, 1986). Heavy metal pollution originating mainly from industrial discharges carries the risk of seafood contamination and human poisoning as experienced at Minamata Bay, Japan, with industrial effluents containing methyl-mercury (Piotrowski and Inskip, 1981; Huss

1988). Various forms of shellfish poisoning in humans such as PSP (paralytic shellfish poisoning), NSP (neurotoxic shellfish poisoning), DSP (diarrhoeic shellfish poisoning, ASP (amnesic shellfish poisoning) are occurring worldwide due to consumption of shellfish which accumulated phycotoxins stemming from toxic algal blooms. Effects of poisoning include gastro-intestinal disorders, respiratory paralysis, memory loss and death (WHO, 1984).

78. In summarizing, the potential negative implications of ecological degradation affecting directly or indirectly the socio-economic conditions within the environment of coastal aquaculture would include the following:

- decline in quality and quantity of food fish both cultured and captured,
- increased human health risks and reduced nutritional status,
- reduced consumer confidence and decreasing fish marketability within local, national and international environments,
- increasing resource-user conflicts and growing competition for markets and credits,
- decline and failures (collapse) of aquaculture enterprises and/or other fishery practices (e.g., artisanal fisheries) including the post-harvest sector, and

social disruption within the rural environment following:

  - displacement of traditional community-based activities in agriculture, forestry and fisheries;
  - decreasing employment opportunities; shift towards unskilled and seasonal labour;
  - marginalization of resident resource-users and non-resource users due to increasing income distribution changes;
  - migration towards urban centres.

# 4. FACTORS INFLUENCING ENVIRONMENTAL PERFORMANCE OF COASTAL AQUACULTURE

79. An account follows on important factors which affect the environmental compatibility of coastal aquaculture. The perspective provided here is on factors which determine technical appropriateness, economic viability and social acceptability (Chong, 1990b). A consideration of these factors is crucial for coastal aquaculture in terms of sustainable development of the industry as well as for successful implementation of each aquaculture venture. These factors should not be considered in isolation but simultaneously since they are, in most cases, closely interrelated.

## The site

80. Space is required, both on land and/or water. The most important site factors (Huguenin and Colt, 1989) are listed in **Table 12**. Seawater properties defining most water quality requirements for aquaculture purposes are listed in **Table 13**. The site will determine availability of water, of which considerable volumes (both sea- and fresh-water) may be needed to maintain water quality. Hydrographic and topographic site characteristics are very important, in particular for sea-based and land-based farms relying on natural water movements (currents, tides) for adequate water exchange and waste dispersal. Lifespan, possibilities for expansion and intensification, and the ecological effect of an aquafarm are often determined by physical characteristics of the site selected. However, the ecological characteristics of the site, e.g., diversity, structure, dynamics and interrelationships of benthic and pelagic communities may be quite distinct. The level and extent of ecological change may, therefore, vary from site to site.

## The species

81. Coastal aquaculture organisms differ significantly in their biological and eco-physiological characteristics. Reproduction, feeding habits, food and nutritional requirements, behaviour, growth capacities, water quality requirements, stress tolerance and susceptibility to parasites and disease characterize suitability of a species to be cultured. The very specific characteristics of the cultured organisms also determine type, magnitude and range of ecological implications. Biological interactions between cultured organisms and wild communities may also be restricted to the immediate vicinity of the site, or affect wider areas.

## The culture method

82. The choice of the culture method will, to some extent, depend on species and site selected. Availability and affordability of resources and inputs (land, water, seed, fertilizers/feeds, energy, skills) will also govern the ease or difficulty with which a site can be developed for extensive, semi-intensive or intensive aquaculture. Major factors in environmental performance of aquafarms are design and construction of facilities as well as the operative efficiency in the production process.

### (a) *Design and construction*

83. Since "ideal" aquaculture sites may not always be available, it will be the ability for adaptive design and engineering which will significantly determine productivity and environmental compatibility of an aquafarm. Technical soundness of construction and setting of holding units, type and amount of materials used, disposal of removed soil and vegetation, are important factors of ecological relevance. Similarly important are the set-up of systems for water renewal and waste water discharge in land-based aquafarms. For water exchange in sea-based farms, anchorage, size of nets and their meshes, seabed coverage, distance between stakes, etc., have to be considered in relation to water depth, bottom slope and exposure to prevailing currents. Clearly, the expected biomass of a farm will determine the magnitude of waste output and water exchange requirements. Unfortunately, the varying degrees of susceptibility of the environment to degradation are often not considered when planning and designing an aquafarm.

**Table 12:** Important bio-physical factors in aquaculture site selection (modified from Huguenin and Colt, 1989)

Biological Environment
* Primary Productivity: phostosynthetic activity.
* Local Ecology: number of trophic levels, dominant species.
* Wild populations of desired species: adults, sources of seed stocks.
* Presence and Concentrations of Predators: land, water, airborne.
* Endemic diseases and Parasites.

Locational Factors
* Watershed Characteristics: area gradients (elevations and distances), ground cover, runoff, up-gradient activities.
* Ground Water Supply: aquifers, water table depth, quality.
* Tides: ranges, rates, seasonal and storm variations, oscillations.
* Waves: amplitude, wave length, direction, seasonal and storm variations, storm frequency.
* Coastal Currents: magnitude, direction and seasonal variations.
* Existing Facilities and characteristics.
* Accessibility of site.
* History of Site: prior uses and experiences.

Soil Factors
* Soil Type, Profile, Subsoil Characteristics.
* Percolation Rate: coefficient of hydraulic permeability.
* Topography and distribution of soil types.
* Particle Size and Shape.
* Angle of Repose: wet, dry.
* Fertility
* Microbiogical Population
* Leachable Toxins: pesticides, heavy metals, other chemicals.

Meteorological Factors
* Winds: prevailing directions, velocities, seasonal variations, storm intensity and frequency.
* Light: total annual solar energy impingement, intensity, quality, photoperiod: diurnal cycle.
* Air Temperature and variations.
* Relative Humidity or Dew Point and variations.
* Precipitation: amount, annual distribution, storm maxima and frequency.

**Table 13:** Seawater properties important in aquaculture water quality management (modified from Huguenin and Colt, 1989)

Physical Parameters
* Temperature Range (daily and seasonal variability)
* Salinity Range (tidal and seasonal variability)
* Particulates (solids)
  - composition (organic and inorganic)
  - size
  - concentration
* Color
* Light
  - artificial or natural
  - total annual incident energy
  - intensity of radiant energy
  - quality of light
  - photoperiod (daily cycles)

Chemical Parameters
* pH and Alkalinity
* Gases
  - total gas pressure
  - oxygen
  - nitrogen
  - carbon dioxide
  - hydrogen sulfide
* Nutrients
  - nitrogen compounds
  - phosphorus compounds
  - trace metals and speciation
* Organic Coumpounds
  - biodegradable
  - non-biodegradable
* Toxic Coumpounds
  - heavy metals
  - biocides

Biological Parameters
* Bacteria (type and concentrations)
* Virus
* Fungi
* Others

(b) *Operation*

84. Preparation and maintenance of holding units, technical installations (e.g., sluice gates, pumps), equipment (e.g., aerators, feeders) and gear (e.g., harvesting nets, boats) is essential. Fluctuation in the availability of good quality seed for stocking often results in inefficient use of farm facilities. In contrast, over-stocking, i.e., high stocking density combined with low water exchange, may, however, reduce growth and create water quality and health problems. Inadequate farm operation often directly affects stress level and required water- (and soil-) quality. Ensuing increased susceptibility to diseases and parasites may then lead to excessive use of prophylactic drugs. Similar problems can be expected with over-use of fertilizers and feeds. Of importance is also the type (physico-chemical characteristics) of fertilizers applied and feeds given. Further, feeding method, (in particular frequency, timing, dispersal of food) and particle size determine the amount of food eaten. In short, efficient farm management, which includes rational choice and utilization of inputs as well as adequate timing and phasing of farm operations, can significantly influence magnitude and extent of ecological effects, and costs.

(c) *Production level*

85. It may be expected that individual, small-scale aquaculture practices with comparatively low yields have little or no significant effect on the surrounding ecosystem. However, production levels have been increased through expansion (increase in culture area) and intensification of culture operations or inputs. Both factors, expansion and intensification, carry an enhanced potential for adverse ecological effect.

Skills

86. In some cases, aquaculturists lack technical, managerial and practical skills to efficiently operate their aquafarms. Skilled labour is sometimes imported. Appropriate aquaculture manpower is an important factor determining farm productivity.

Technological standard

87. Present aquaculture technologies are, in many cases, far from complete and still require substantial improvements to ensure reliability, efficiency and easy application. Application of appropriate and adaptive technology can improve environmental performance of aquafarms.

Access to financing and credit

88. Small-scale farms often do not have the financial resources to afford improvements in farm management efficiency and productivity through appropriate technology, including adequate quality of seed, fertilizers/feed and equipment. Moreover, small-scale investors facing serious problems in obtaining credit have little flexibility in selecting and developing appropriate sites.

Economic viability

89. Long-term economic viability is often restricted due to increasing costs of required resources or inputs available in the area where the aquafarm is sited. As a result, it becomes increasingly difficult for the aquafarmer to optimize the utilization of inputs, to improve the quality of products, to lower production costs, and to reduce adverse ecological effect. Marketing costs (including costs of transportation of products) can be considerable. Fluctuations in prices of aquaculture products seem to particularly affect profitability of extensive (low-input, low-productivity) systems as well as intensive systems with high capital investment and production costs. Frequent collapse and abandonment of aquafarms due to financial and economic feasibility constraints, may lead to sceptcism about social acceptability and environmental compatibility of coastal aquaculture practices.

Legal status

90. Many aquafarmers and aquaculture investors often face legal uncertainties about the utilization of land and water resources required. Often, there are many authorities having direct and indirect jurisdiction over the use of land and water for aquaculture, which causes confusion and heavy bureaucratic burdens to the aquafarmer. The type of tenurial arrangements, such as short- or long-term leases of land or water surface, can influence development and lifespan of aquafarms. Uncertainties in the allocation of land and water resources under public domain in many cases result in social conflicts with other users. Environmental legislation, if existing, often does not cover specific requirements and characteristics of the various coastal aquaculture practices.

Coordination

91. Coordination of coastal aquaculture development supported by adequate information bases and planning capacities, is lacking in many countries. Even though aquaculture development may be prioritized in national development plans, technical assistance to the sector and enforcement of supportive regulations is frequently not being carried out due to lack of financial resources. Inadequate institutional cooperation between government authorities in charge of planned development of the various activities in the coastal zone (agriculture, fisheries, urban and industrial development, sanitation, etc.) may significantly hamper both overall development as well as environment protection efforts.

# 5. ASSESSMENT OF ENVIRONMENTAL HAZARDS AND IMPACTS OF COASTAL AQUACULTURE

92. In this section, general issues of marine pollution assessment are addressed (5.1). Selected aquaculture-specific methods for pollution assessment are then presented (5.2). Last, the role and functions of environmental impact assessment (EIA) are described (5.3).

## 5.1 General Considerations on Marine Pollution Assessment

93. Within the context of coastal aquaculture development and environment, it appears to be important and useful to address definitions and concepts related to marine pollution assessment and prevention.

*Marine pollution*

94. GESAMP gives following definition of marine pollution (GESAMP, 1991b):

> *"Marine pollution means the introduction by man, directly or indirectly, of substances or energy into the marine environment (including estuaries) resulting in such deleterious effects as harm to living resources, hazards to human health, hindrance to marine activities including fishing, impairment of quality for use of sea water and reduction of amenities."*

### 5.1.1 Environmental capacity

95. GESAMP further advocates the environmental capacity concept (GESAMP, 1986; Pravdic, 1987). The environmental (also known as receiving, absorptive or assimilative) capacity is defined as a property of the environment, a measurement of its ability to accommodate a particular activity or rate of an activity, such as the discharge of contaminants, without unacceptable impact: it is the "ability of a receiving system or ecosystem to cope with certain concentrations or levels of waste discharges without suffering any significant deleterious effects" (Cairns, 1977, 1989).

96. An important characteristic of both, the above marine pollution definition and the environmental capacity concept, is the discrimination between "contamination", meaning increased presence of substances in the environment as a result of human activities but with no significant adverse effects, and "pollution", signifying the occurrence of adverse effects. The distinction between the terms is important since it implies that environmental change resulting from human activities may, or may not, be judged to have adverse effects. The boundary between these two regimes requires a definition of "acceptability". Irrespective of where this boundary is drawn, the concept of acceptable change remains valid.

97. The environmental capacity approach works well as an interactive environmental management strategy. Other traditionally-used complex strategies, based on environmental quality objectives or simple but readily enforceable strategies - such as those based on uniform emission standards, maximum allowable concentrations in effluent, the black/grey/white lists or the application of principles of best practicable means available - are considered as simple components of this adaptive, interactive strategy. A short description/discussion of traditionally-used strategies is given in **Annex 3**.

98. Assessing the environmental capacity is a scientific approach which requires technical and socio-economic inputs as parallel, interactive and complementary activities in decision-making in integral, environmentally compatible, development planning. It emphasizes the objectivity and independence of technical inputs and their influences on decisions related to socio-economic feasibility. It also emphasizes that the acceptability of environmental impact rests on much more than political considerations. Such acceptability can be determined scientifically, assuming that the environmental capacity can be quantified. The environmental capacity approach seeks to define the

critical load and in its application seeks to keep actual inputs as far as practicable below this. Once the environmental capacity of a given substance is determined, it can be apportioned for various resource uses and needs.

99. The methodology for the assessment of the environmental capacity, which is site- and contaminant-specific, uses critical pathway analysis for both conservative and non-conservative contaminants and establishment of environmental quality objectives, criteria and standards. Faced with the inevitability of several sources of uncertainties in real situations, a probabilistic approach is used as an alternative to deterministic analysis. The approach proposed is decision analysis. The methodology recommended (GESAMP, 1986) consists of three decision-stages (see **Figure 8**). Socio-economic goals (priorities and objectives) are assessed in the planning stage, considering present and future use of resources. In the preliminary scientific assessment stage the environmental capacity is derived and quantified, resulting in the setup of allowable inputs. Finally, monitoring provides a continuous test of whether the environmental capacity is balanced, exceeded or underutilized. Consequently, adaptive and/or corrective measures may be required.

100. In this context, the role of science is to assess and predict man-induced environmental change. The key scientific issues and disciplines required can be grouped into two categories:

(a) the sources, transport, transformation, and fate of substances introduced to the marine environment

In this category, the distribution of substances is related to their sources, which involves physical, chemical and biological science with major emphasis on physical and chemical oceanography. Readers interested in the state-of-the-art of coastal modelling in relation to transport, dispersion and fate of contaminants disposed of in the coastal environment are referred to GESAMP (1991a).

(b) the effects of these substances on organisms, including man, and resources and amenities in the marine environment

This second category involves the translation of resulting exposures into their effects on organisms, man and amenities, which are covered primarily by studies on toxicology and biological effects.

Parameters

101. Any evaluation for a potentially harmful chemical substance must take into account two types of factors, the first intrinsic with the substance, the second related to the extrinsic conditions and their reciprocal interactions. Basically, the necessary scientific parameters are:

**Quantity:** production, uses, discharge patterns, loads, sources

**Distribution:** physico-chemical characteristics, affinity for environmental compartments

**Persistence:** kinetics of hydrolysis, photolysis, biodegradation

**Bioaccumulation:** n-octanol/water partition coefficient, metabolic pathways in different organisms

**Toxicity:** measures of biological activity of the substance (ideally from cells to ecosystems)

**Ecosystem typologies:** biotic and abiotic characteristics and structure and functions of ecosystems

**Time-scale of events**

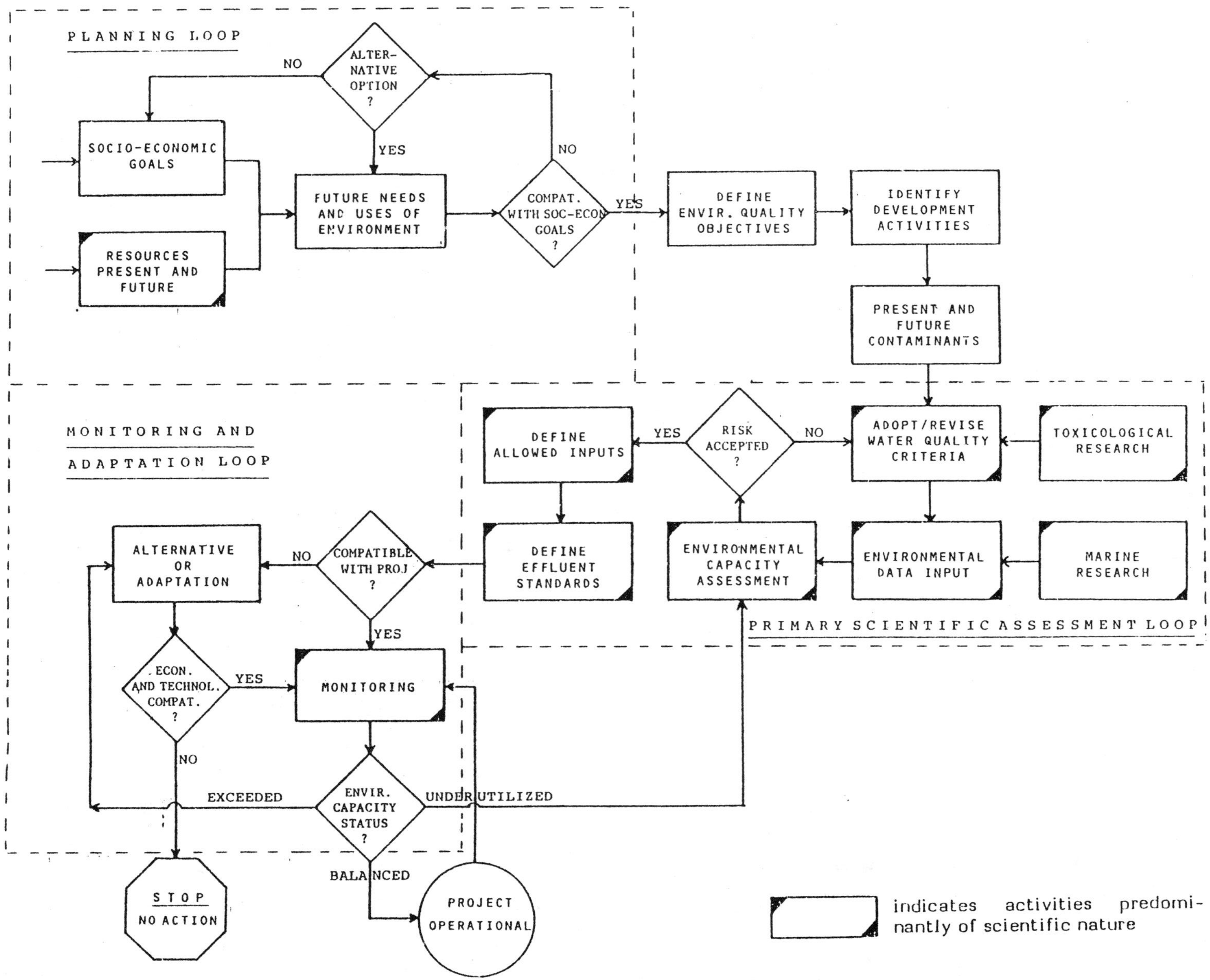


**Figure 8**: Methodology for the assessment of the impact of pollutants on the marine environment (from GESAMP, 1986)

Impact prediction

102. Within the environmental capacity approach, hazard assessment (Landner, 1989, 1988; Bro-Rasmussen and Christiansen, 1984) is a key scientific tool for predicting potentially adverse effects of the discharge of pollutants on the basis of both their inherent properties and the probability of exposure to such substances which determines environmental damage to organisms. In other words, hazard assessment is based on the relationship of the expected environmental concentration of a chemical substance (to which target organisms are potentially exposed) and the toxicological properties of the substance, i.e., the predicted concentrations with adverse biological effect (Cairns *et al.,* 1978). The prediction of the environmental concentration starts with the determination of exposure-related data, which refers to the rate of chemical substance input, the properties of the substance and the environment. The persistence and the distribution of the substance are evaluated from data on physico-chemical characteristics, biogeochemical behavior, biodegradability, bioaccumulation potential and bioavailability. Biological effects are predicted on the basis of acute and chronic toxicity studies or are calculated on the basis of quantitative structure activity relationships (QSARs) (Könemann, 1981; Halfon, 1989; Boudou and Ribeyre, 1989; Lloyd, 1991a, 1991b).

103. In summarizing, the hazard assessment process should yield clear predictions of (1) the transport pathways and rates, (2) the likely environment compartment (water, sediment and/or biota) where the substance/material is likely to accumulate and (3) the likely effect of the substance/material at a given target site or on a given organism or set of organisms. However, predictions should be made not only of chemical concentrations but also of acceptable biological effects. Limits to changes in either a stress response of a given species and/or a community response should be clearly stated. Regulatory measures may then be adopted upon comparison of the predicted environmental concentration (in water, sediments and organisms) and the information on lowest concentration where adverse biological effects can be expected.

### 5.1.2 Monitoring

104. Through monitoring, experts can provide coastal resource users and administrators involved in environmental management with information on:

(a) whether the condition of the environment is improving or deteriorating;
(b) whether any contemplated management activity, be it for development of a sector other than fisheries or fisheries or aquaculture itself, has had an impact on the environment;
(c) whether individual operators are complying with regulatory requirements.

105. The design of any monitoring programme should be based on clearly-defined objectives and the formulation of testable hypotheses. Monitoring is essential to verify impact predictions in any hazard assessment exercise. It must also be recognized that monitoring in most cases has to be a long-term exercise to be useful and efficient. Since monitoring can be very costly, data should only be collected that:

(a) are required to satisfy the objectives;
(b) are amenable to meaningful interpretation; and
(c) have known precision and accuracy.

106. Otherwise, technical and financial resources will be wasted and, in the case of compliance monitoring, the production of data of doubtful quality may limit their legal acceptance.

107. More specifically, adequate ecological monitoring requires:

(a) the measurement of (i) contaminant levels, (ii) extent of physical modification and/or (iii) related effects on the environment;

(b) the measurement of the rate of contaminant input or of frequency and dynamics of physical modification;

(c) the measurement of effects on identified target(s) exposed to environmental change.

108. Monitoring programmes should include both physico-chemical and biological aspects so that where possible measured biological responses can be related to specific chemical doses and/or physical modification.

109. The success of monitoring depends on the implementation of a strong quality assurance programme. A quality assurance programme has two basic components. The first, quality control, includes activities designed to ensure that the sampling and analytical techniques are adequate for the intended purpose. This forms the basis for deciding if a monitoring programme is adequate to significantly detect assumed (predicted) changes. The second, quality assessment, provides an ongoing basis by which the quality of data is maintained at the required level. This is accomplished through the use of standardized procedures, standard reference material and inter-laboratory comparisons.

110. Biological monitoring can provide a measurement of the direct effect of adverse water and sediment quality on organisms by assessing the extent to which a specific biological response deviates from a normal value. Measurements of effects the individual organism level include reduced growth rates, susceptibility to disease, or mortality of sensitive life-stages. Measurements of community structure changes can be readily equated with harm, particularly if species of commercial or conservation value have been reduced in number. Biological monitoring should be integrated with chemical monitoring, so that the extent to which the measured effects can be ascribed to specific chemicals can be established. This is true also of the monitoring of those chemicals that can be accumulated in the tissues of organisms, particularly those harvested for human consumption. The main objective here is to evaluate the concentrations found in the context of relevant acceptable daily intakes. But the data should also provide information on the potential harmfulness of such concentrations to the organisms themselves. At present, many concentration-effect relationships established for organisms are based on levels of chemicals in the ambient water and not on the amounts accumulated in the tissues.

111. Surveillance differs from monitoring in that predictions are not tested but target sites or organisms are surveyed to ascertain whether or not there are detectable differences between the surveyed site and control site.

112. However, the systematic collection of first-hand information on apparent pollution events or other visible environmental deterioration by fishermen and aquaculture operators may - in some cases - prove very useful for various purposes such as:

- early detection/early warning schemes (e.g., on oil spills, phytoplankton blooms)

- preliminary demarcation of pollution-exposed areas (e.g., changing patterns of distribution/expansion of contamination)

- record-keeping of chronology/history of events (frequency, duration, time of year, etc.)

113. Such activities, which may be better termed "regular observation" or "watchkeeping" of the environment, could eventually support ecological surveillance and/or monitoring programmes.

## 5.2 Selected Aquaculture-Specific Pollution Assessment Methods

114. When assessing environmental change resulting from aquaculture, it is important to distinguish between:

(a) output (waste load) and consumption (e.g., of oxygen, particulate material, phytoplankton) by culture practices or organisms; and
(b) related ecological effects.

115. For example, the quantification of the total suspended solids that might be generated by an aquaculture operation does not equate to the effect that such output might have on the ecology of the farm site. Unfortunately, this interaction is often discussed as though the two issues were the same.

116. Selected aquaculture-specific pollution assessment methods are described below. It is emphasized that environmental impact assessment methods are being improved (see Silvert, in press).

### 5.2.1 Mass balance estimates of waste production

117. So far, most estimates of waste production have been published for temperate carnivorous fish species, in particular salmonids. A graphic illustration of the fate of waste material released from intensive fish farming is given in **Figure 9**. It is possible to estimate the amounts of uneaten food, faeces and excreta produced from data on feed qualities and quantities, food conversion ratio (FCR) values, digestibilities and faecal composition, and to produce mass balance equations for various waste parameters, such as nitrogen, phosphorus or carbon, solids or biological oxygen demand (Beveridge *et al.*, 1991).

118. Some general equations follow (modified from Iwama, 1991) which enable the estimations to be made of the output of the total mass of particulate organic matter deriving from uneaten food and faeces.

Given:

| | | |
|---|---|---|
| UW | = | percentage uncaptured feed waste/100 (i.e., ratio of total food uncaptured to total food fed) |
| F | = | percentage faecal waste/100 (i.e., ratio of total faecal waste to total food eaten) |
| FCR | = | food conversion ratio (weight of food fed/weight gained) |
| PD | = | production (increase in fish biomass) |
| O | = | total output of particulate organic matter |

Then:

| | | | | |
|---|---|---|---|---|
| TF | = | total food fed | = | PD x FCR |
| TU | = | total food uncaptured | = | TF x UW |
| TE | = | total food eaten | = | TF - TU |
| TFW | = | total faecal waste | = | F x TE |
| O | = | TU + TFW | | |

119. The total amount of food fed (TF), if unknown, can be derived from estimates for production (PD) and FCR values. The significance of FCR values (and water content in feeds and fish) for waste production estimates are discussed by Hopkins and Manci (1989). FCR values from cages appear higher than those from ponds, possibly indicating higher food losses (Beveridge, 1984). There have been few attempts to estimate directly the proportion of uneaten food (UW), partly because it is difficult to distinguish between the food and the faecal components of solids collected. Estimated values for UW can range from 1 to 30% or more. Faecal waste production can be estimated from studies on the digestibility of main diet components. Dry weight based estimates for whole diet digestibilities seem to compare well with values for F, which range from 25 to 30%.

120. With the total content of carbon, nitrogen and phosphorus in feeds and faeces known, it is possible to estimate the output of each of these components in the uneaten food and faeces fractions using following general equations:

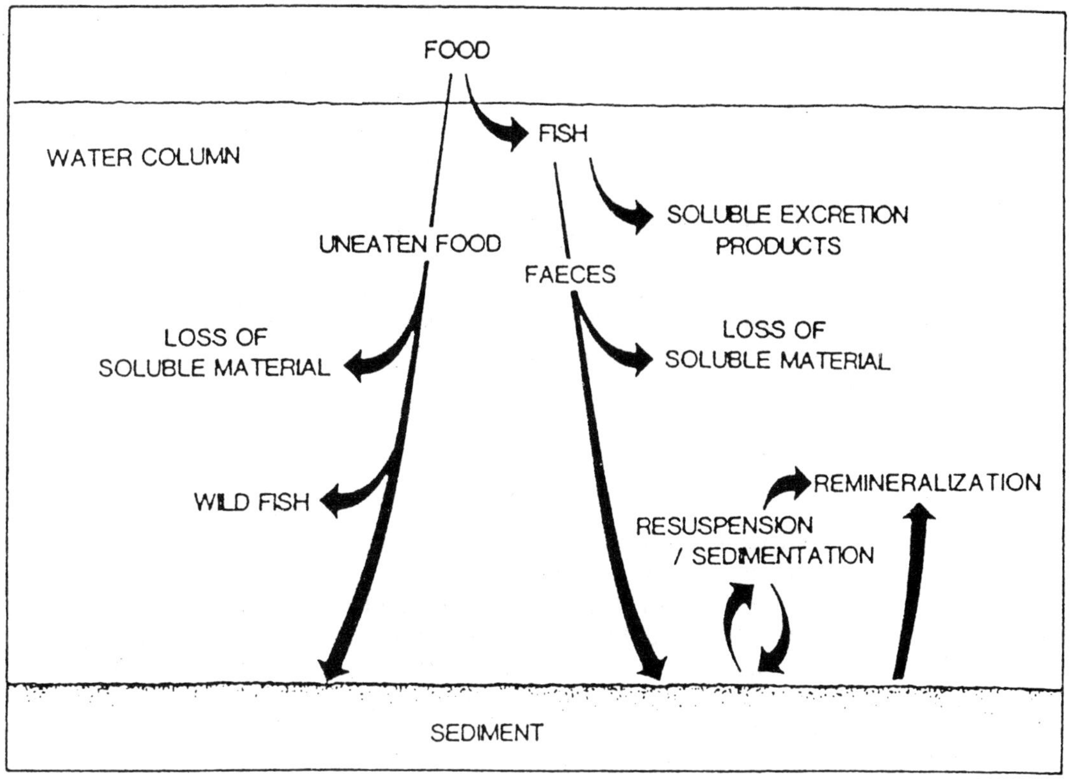


**Figure 9:** The fate of waste material released from intensive fish farming (from Gowen *et al.,* 1990)

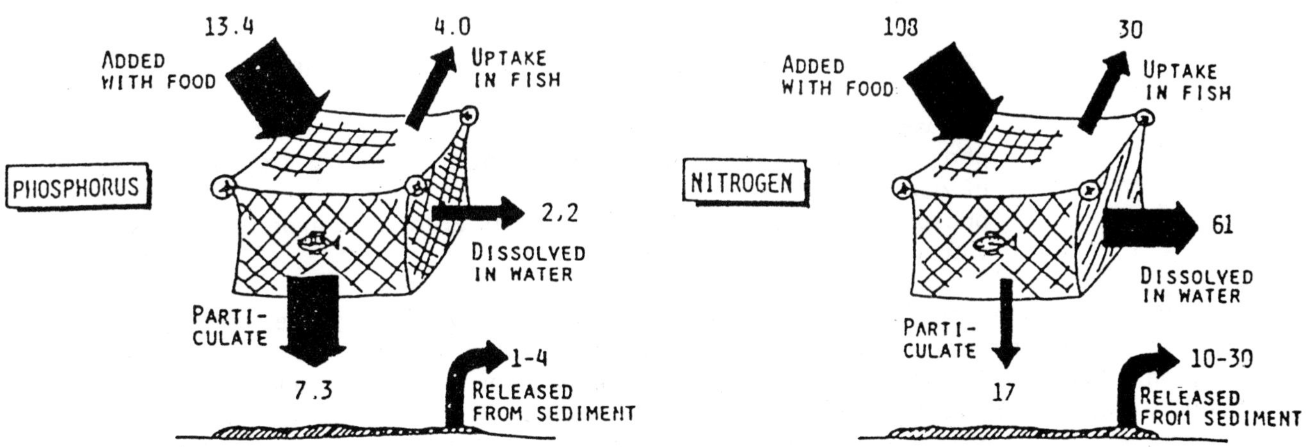


**Figure 10:** Phosphorus and nitrogen load from cage fish farming, expressed in kg per ton produced fish per season. The feed coefficient used is 1.5 and the content of phosphorus and nitrogen in the feed is considered to be 0.9% and 7.2% of wet weight, respectively. The desorption from the sediment is considered to be 50% of the sedimented (particulate) phosphorus and nitrogen (Enell and Ackefors, 1991)

UM = mass of C, N, or P output from uncaptured food
UM = TF x UW x K
EM = mass of C, N, or P output from eaten food
EM = (TF - TU) x K x E
TM = total mass of C, N, or P output from both uncaptured and captured food
TM = UM + EM

where:

K = percentage of each component in food/100
E = percentage of each component in faeces/100

121. Given the total content of a component in the fish, the output of this component can also be estimated as being equivalent to the difference between the content of the component in the food and that retained in the fish. Wallin and Hakanson (1991) give following equation to estimate the nutrient load from fish farms:

$$L = P \times (FC \times C_{feed} - C_{fish})$$

where:

L = nitrogen and phosphorus load (kg tot-N & tot-P/year)
P = fish production (kg wet weight/year)
FC = feed coefficient (kg wet weight feed/kg fish production)
$C_{feed}$ = nitrogen and phosphorus concentration in feed (% wet weight)
$C_{fish}$ = nitrogen and phosphorus concentration in fish (% wet weight)

122. A slightly different and perhaps more detailed description of these relationships is presented by Ackefors and Enell (1990):

The equation for the phosphorus load is:

$$\text{kg P} = (A \times C_{dp}) - (B \times C_{fp})$$

The equation for the nitrogen load is:

$$\text{kg N} = (A \times C_{dn}) - (B \times C_{fn})$$

where:

A = wet weight of dry pellets used per year (normal water content in dry pellets is 8-10%)
B = wet weight of fish produced per year
$C_d$ = phosphorus ($C_{dp}$) and nitrogen ($C_{dn}$) content of dry pellets, expressed as % of wet weight
$C_f$ = phosphorus ($C_{fp}$) and nitrogen ($C_{fn}$) content of the fish, expressed as % of wet weight

123. In summarizing, these general mass balance equations serve to roughly estimate waste production from fish farms (see **Figures 10 and 11**). It must be noted, however, that they are based mainly on a number of assumptions (e.g., when accounting for feed losses) and results from laboratory studies (e.g., estimations of digestibilities). Additional aspects need to be considered such as diurnal and seasonal variability, variations between different species, effects of temperature, body size, health, feeding rates, quality of nutritional components, synergistic/antagonistic effects of one dietary component on the digestibility of another, influence of processing and non-nutritional constituents on digestibility. Further, culture system and management factors will also influence waste load composition, for example, in terms of suspended or settleable solids, anc nitrogen or phosphorus species.

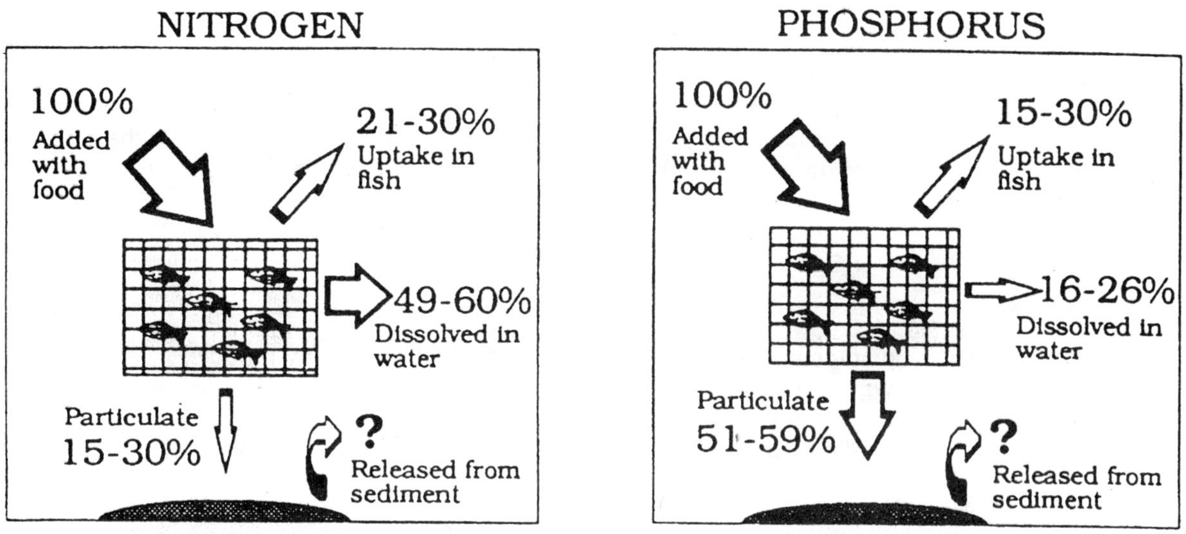


Figure 11: Mass balance for nitrogen and phosphorus flow in a fish farm (from Wallin and Hakanson, 1991)

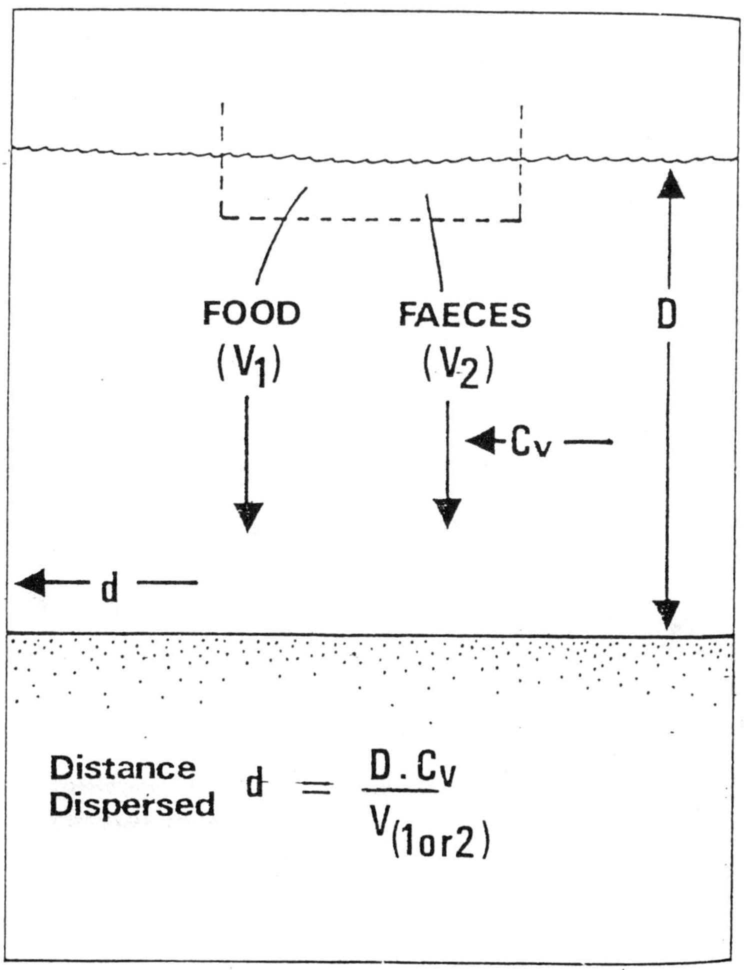


Figure 12: The diagrammatic representation of the horizontal displacement of organic waste showing the relationship between water depth, current velocity, and settling velocity of waste particles (from Gowen *et al.*, 1989)

### 5.2.2 Modelling organic enrichment of the benthos

124. The dispersal and loading of particulate organic waste to the sediment will depend on the amount of waste produced, surface area of the farm, water depth, current velocity, and the settling of the waste particles. Estimates for the waste-loading over a potential area affected can be derived (Gowen *et al.,* 1989) from following equation (see also **Figure 12**):

$$d = D \times C_v / V_{(1 \text{ or } 2)}$$

where:

| | | |
|---|---|---|
| $d$ | = | distance dispersed (horizontal distance travelled by particle) |
| $D$ | = | water depth |
| $C_v$ | = | current speed |
| $V$ | = | settling velocity of waste particles (uneaten food and faeces) |

125. It is important to distinguish between uneaten food and faeces particles since the settling velocities of the two are different. In practice, however, it is likely that there is a broad size and density spectrum of waste particles and hence settling velocities. Particles may also break down into smaller particles. Variations in current speed and direction are accounted for in the model by Gowen *et al.* (1989). Other limitations are due to lack of consideration of various aspects such as possible consumption of uneaten food by wild fish, possible resuspension of sedimented material, differences in bottom characteristics, effects of benthic organisms and other microbiological and chemical processes on the deposited organic particulate matter (Holmer, 1991; Holmer and Kristensen, 1992).

### 5.2.3 Assessment of effects on the benthic ecosystem

126. There is a variety of benthological methods to assess physico-chemical changes and biological responses resulting from organic enrichment (see for example Viarengo and Canesi (1991); Frid and Mercer (1989); O'Connor *et al.* (1989).

<u>Bottom types</u>

127. The occurrence of organic enrichment effects will depend on conditions of bottom dynamics and water exchange, which determine sediment types. Hakanson *et al.* (1988) give methods for determination of bottom dynamics conditions and suggest the following classification of bottom types which reflect the influence of wave action and prevailing currents in coastal areas:

(a) areas of erosion (E) dominate where there is no apparent deposition of fine materials (i.e., bottoms of sand, gravel, consolidated clays and/or rocks, so-called erosion bottoms);
(b) areas of transportation (T) prevail where fine materials are deposited periodically (i.e., bottoms of mixed sediments, so-called transportation bottoms)
(c) areas of accumulation (A) prevail where fine materials are deposited continuously (i.e., soft bottoms; so-called accumulation bottoms).

128. Accumulation bottoms are often characteristic of sheltered coastal areas where many aquafarms are located. On A-bottoms, where the organic matter is deposited over a rather long period, effects of oxygen depletion are frequent, and it is to be expected that the bottom fauna is more severely affected than it would be on other sediment types. Organic matter released on T-bottoms spreads further, and the effect, although likely to be less severe, is dispersed over a larger area.

<u>Sediment metabolism</u>

129. Physico-chemical parameters measured in investigations included current speeds, sedimentation rates using sediment traps, sediment thickness and density, sediment particle size,

sediment chemistry of the solid phase and pore waters (water content, dissolved oxygen content, content of inorganic and organic, soluble and particulate components, alkalinity, redox potential) and near-bottom water chemistry (dissolved oxygen content, release of nutrients such as ammonium, nitrate, phosphate and gases such as hydrogen sulphide and methane).

130. Based on physico-chemical parameters measured, sediment metabolism patterns have been analysed which indicate complex chemical processes combined with aerobic and anaerobic microbial activities. It can be stated that high, localized deposition rates of particulate organic matter are associated with metabolically very active sediments. The microbial activity is stimulated and the demand for oxygen in microbial processes and for re-oxidation of reduced mineralization products increases to the extent of oxygen depletion resulting in a net production from the sediment of the by-products of anaerobic metabolism (ammonium, hydrogen sulphide and methane). The reader interested in further discussion on related effects and methodologies is referred to Holmer (1991); Holmer and Kristensen (1992); Weston and Gowen (1988); Kupka-Hansen *et al.* (1991); Kaspar *et al.* (1988); Lumb (1989).

Effects on benthic fauna

131. Bottom fauna living in and above sediments can be used as an indicator in aquaculture pollution studies, since the benthos is fairly stationary.

132. Bottom fauna community structures can be disturbed by organic enrichment of the sediment to the extent of complete disappearance of macrofauna. It is generally assumed that a macrobenthic community subject to increased organic loading, either spatially or temporally, will exhibit (Weston, 1990):

(a) a decrease in species richness and an increase in the total number of individuals as a result of the high densities of a few opportunistic species;
(b) a general reduction in biomass, although there may be an increase in biomass corresponding to a dense assemblage of opportunists;
(c) a decrease in body size of the average species or individual;
(d) a shallowing of that portion of the sediment column occupied by infauna;
(e) shifts in the relative dominance of trophic guilds.

133. Several methods can be used to analyse changes in bottom community structures. For example, an area can be divided into different pollution zones using the biomass and abundance values and the occurrence of indicator species, which exhibit specific reactions to organic pollution. Often, so-called SAB curves are used (Weston, 1991), which display the changes in species number, abundance and biomass along a gradient of organic pollution (see **Figure 13**). A variety of diversity indices is in common usage (Shannon-Wiener index, evenness, Sanders rarefraction technique). Disturbance at individual sites may be determined by plotting the number of individuals in geometric classes of abundance, or by the abundance, biomass comparison (ABC) method whereby the cumulative dominance in terms of abundance and biomass are plotted against a logarithmic scale of species rank.

134. It should be noted that most methods have advantages and limitations in the assessment of aquaculture pollution effects on the benthos. Results from related studies are, in some cases, variable. Quantitative appraisal of parameters of benthic community changes may, in some cases, be difficult. And, changes, when occurring, are not always attributable to organic enrichment. Prediction of ecological effects however appears to be possible in qualitative terms based on empiric evidence. For further reference on benthological studies, see Gray *et al.* (1992); Lauren-Maatta *et al.* (1991); Holmer (1991); Weston (1991); Weston (1990); Brown *et al.* (1987).

### 5.2.4 Modelling hypernutrification and eutrophication

135. Hypernutrification (nutrient enrichment) and eutrophication (increase in primary production)

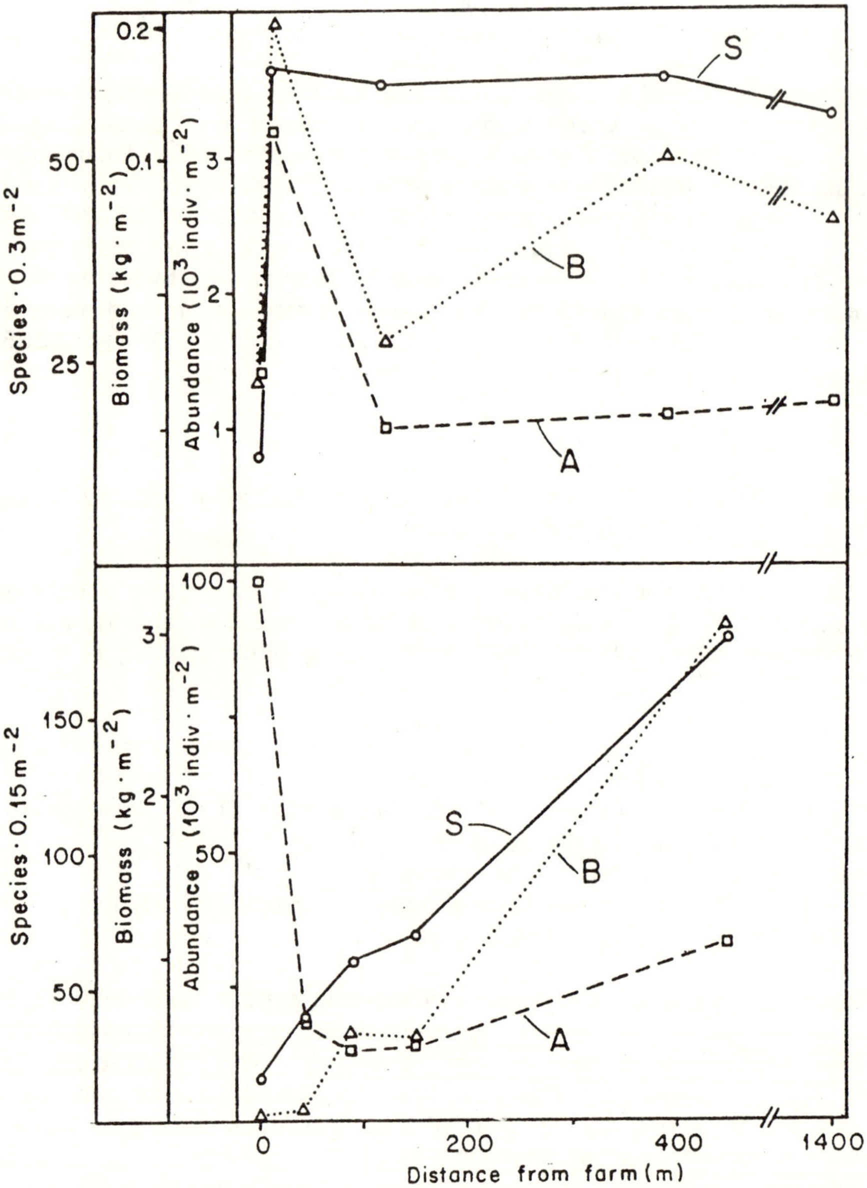


**Figure 13:** Trends in areal species richness (S), biomass (B) and abundance (A) of macrofauna with distance from two salmon net-cage mariculture sites. Data in upper figure from Loch Spelve, Scotland, from Brown *et al.* (1987). Data in lower figure from Puget Sound, northwestern United States, from Weston (1990). (from Weston, 1991)

of open coastal waters due to aquaculture is unlikely, but may occur in semi-enclosed coastal embayments which have restricted water exchange with more open waters.

136. Attempts to model hypernutrification and eutrophication at present appear to be considerably less successful in coastal waters than in inland waters. The same basic principles of relating nutrient concentration to phytoplankton growth together with a dilution or water body-flushing term may apply. However, difficulties in modelling coastal ecosystem responses to nutrient enrichment are generally related to the influence of salinity stratification and tidal mixing, particularly in embayments and estuaries. Also, the boundaries of the affected area are often difficult to define. It is emphasized that, as a consequence of the complex linkages between biological, chemical and physical processes, these models are area-specific and as such their wider use is limited. Despite the range of limitations and the assumptions to be made, such models may be used to provide 'best' and 'worst' case scenarios.

Hypernutrification

137. The extent of hypernutrification depends on the size of the farm and the hydrography of the water body within which the farm is located. Thus the volume of the water body, its rate of exchange with the adjacent sea, the onset and duration of vertical stratification and the extent of horizontal advection, all have an important bearing on the level of hypernutrification.

138. An example for an approximative assessment follows. Assuming complete dispersion of waste nitrogen throughout a semi-enclosed water body, Gowen *et al.* (1989) presented the following approach to estimate the equilibrium increase of soluble nitrogen concentrations:

$$E_c = N \times F/V$$

where:

$E_c$ = equilibrium rise in concentration (level of hypernutrification)
$N$ = daily output of soluble nitrogenous waste
$F$ = flushing time of the waterbody in days
$V$ = volume of the waterbody

Two methods were used for estimating flushing time F or dilution rate D, whereby $D = 1/F$:

(a) Tidal exchange method:

$$D = (V_h - V_l)/T \times V_h$$

where $(V_h - V_l)$ is the volume exchanged every tide, and:

$V_h$ = high water volume of waterbody
$V_l$ = low water volume of waterbody
$T$ = tide period, in days

139. This method assumes that the mean volume of the water body is greater than the tidal volume, which is in turn greater than the volume of river inflow per tide. The method also assumes that there is complete mixing and that none of the water which leaves the basin on the ebb tide returns on the flood, which means that it fails to account for incomplete exchange.

(b) Salinity and river flow method:

$$D = R \times S_o/V(S_o-S)$$

where:

$R$ = rate of river inflow

| | | |
|---|---|---|
| $S_o$ | = | mean salinity of seawater flowing into water body |
| S | = | mean salinity of the outflow |
| V | = | volume of the waterbody |

140. This method assumes a steady state, i.e., uniform river inflow. Direct measurements of ammonium in the water body (in this case a Scottish loch) as well as in the immediate vicinity of the fish farm, however, showed a spatial distribution of ammonium indicating only a very localized hypernutrification around the fish farm.

Eutrophication

141. It is, at present, impossible to predict eutrophication resulting from hypernutrification caused by fish farms. The consequences of hypernutrification in terms of enhanced primary production and phytoplankton standing crop are complex, and respective relationships are still poorly understood. Enhanced primary production could occur without an increase in standing crop, if additional biomass is rapidly removed, for example by grazing. Direct measurements of primary production are therefore likely to be more informative than simple estimates of algal biomass. However, additional nitrogen is not necessarily utilized by phytoplankton. Despite higher levels of hypernutrification, phytoplankton growth might be limited by other factors such as light availability in turbid or deep vertically mixed waters. Hydrographic conditions, such as the flushing time of a water body, can limit the accumulation of phytoplankton biomass, i.e., when algal cells are removed from the source of nitrogen before significant growth occurs. For further discussion on assessment and prediction of potential hypernutrification and eutrophication associated with coastal fish culture, the reader is referred to Gowen and Bradbury (1987); Gowen *et al.* (1989); Gowen *et al.* (1990); Gowen and Ezzi (1992); Wallin and Hakanson (1991); Hakanson and Wallin (1991); Aure and Stigebrandt (1990); Enell and Ackefors (1991); Turrel and Munro (1989).

### 5.2.5 Oxygen depletion

142. The likelihood of large-scale oxygen depletion will clearly depend on size and intensity of the aquaculture operation (i.e., the oxygen demand by both the cultured stock and the wastes released) and the topography/hydrography of the waterbody. An approximative assessment of the holding capacity of the waterbody (i.e., the threshold at which production becomes limited by a non-trophic resource see Rosenthal *et al.* 1988), can be obtained by comparing the oxygen demand of the stock to the pool of available oxygen and the rate of supply. Models to predict effects of aquafarm operations on the oxygen budget of a waterbody are, however, still being developed (see for example Aure and Stigebrandt, 1990).

### 5.2.6 Carrying capacity

143. Shore-based aquaculture practices such as the farming of seaweeds and bivalves interact with coastal food webs since they rely on naturally-available food resources. The carrying capacity of a defined area refers in ecology to the potential maximum production a species or population can maintain in relation to (naturally) available food resources within the area (Rosenthal *et al.,* 1988). Hence, the production potential of, for instance, bivalves in a coastal waterbody is determined by the carrying capacity of this water body. Over-stocking would result in reduced production, since the carrying capacity is exceeded. Carrying capacity can be assessed by evaluating historical records of bivalve culture (see **Figure 14**), by measuring the availability of phytoplankton biomass or by undertaking more detailed studies, e.g., of carbon and nitrogen flows through a bivalve culture unit interacting with the food web (see for example Rodhouse *et al.,* 1985). Methods for estimating the carrying capacity of areas used for oyster and mussel farming are reviewed by Héral (1991).

### 5.2.7 Visual observation and remote sensing of contamination and degradation

144. There are various possibilities to directly or indirectly detect and assess areal extent of

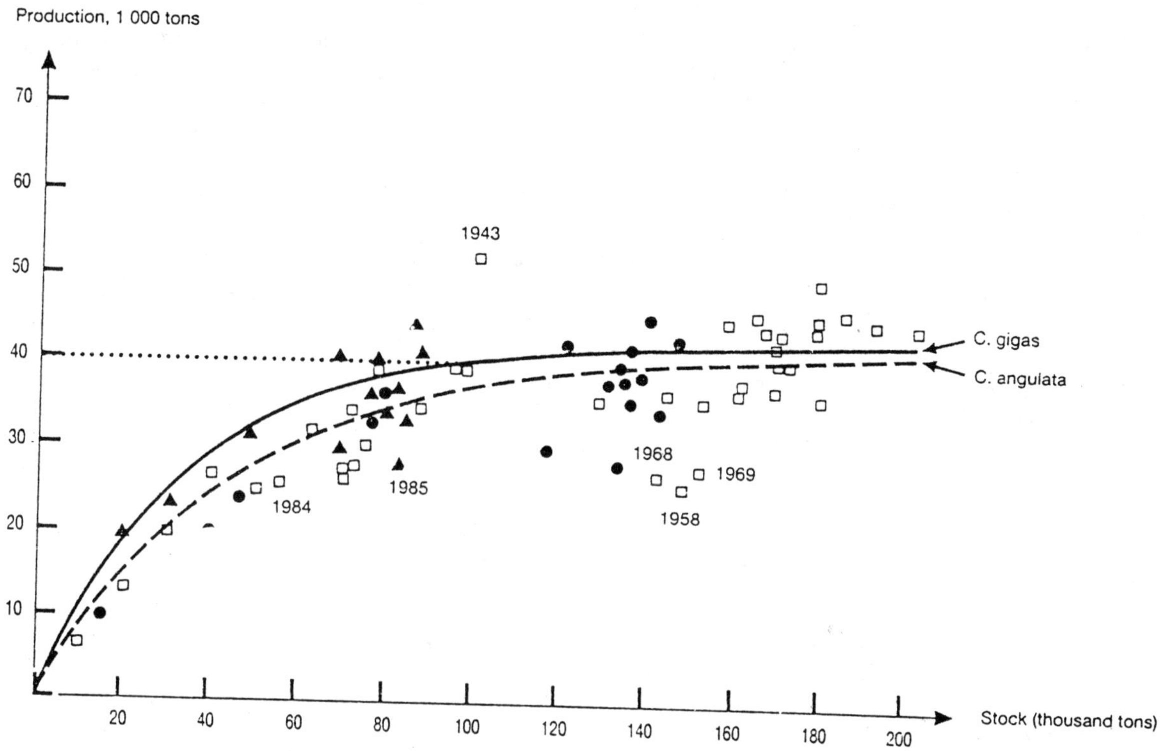


**Figure 14:** Estimated biotic capacity of the Marennes-Oléron basin, France. [Development of oyster production (P) as function of cultured biomass (B) of *Crassostrea gigas* (▲) and *C. angulata* (□). Bullets (●) indicate calculated P/B data for *C. gigas* as equivalent to data of *C. angulata*]. (from Bailly,1989 based on Héral *et al.,* 1986)

contamination and degradation by visual observation and remote sensing.

145. Direct observation of the sediments in the vicinity of aquafarms by divers will give first indications, e.g., on the degree of siltation, on the coverage or damage to benthic flora, on the lack of typical fauna, on the fall-off of shells, on the colour, thickness and consistency of the sediments. For example, a white mat on the sediment surface, formed by the sulphur-oxidizing bacteria *Beggiatoa* is often found around farms. Simple Secchi-disc measurements from boats may reveal degree and extent of turbidity increase in the water column around aquafarms.

146. On a larger scale, aerial photography and video filming may prove useful to record extent of water contamination and degradation of land surface. More sophisticated remote sensing techniques including infra-red and multi-spectral photography, multi-spectral scanning and radiometry, may, under certain circumstances, provide information on effluent discharge plumes, sedimentation patterns, phytoplankton concentrations and changes in coastal land use, all of which may be related to large-scale coastal aquaculture expansion and intensification (Meaden and Kapetsky, 1991; Butler *et al.*, 1988; Kapetsky *et al.*, 1987; FAO, 1989a, 1985b).

147. Large-scale spatial and temporal environmental changes in coastal areas may be assessed using geographical information systems (GIS). A GIS is a computerized approach to storing, manipulating, analysing and reporting data by reference to space (geo-referenced information), i.e., data which can be attributed to a location. GIS has proved useful (see previous citations) *inter alia*: in assessing impacts on aquatic resources and environments from development projects involving land and water use, in aquaculture site selection in relation to ecological and socio-economic variables, in space and resource allocation to conflicting types of use, in aquaculture development planning and environmental impact monitoring.

### 5.2.8 Surveillance and monitoring in coastal aquaculture environments

148. Most coastal aquaculture practices have no or little significant effects on the environment. It can also be expected that, in most cases, the environmental capacity of coastal water bodies is far from being exhausted by the waste load received from aquaculture operations. At present, it is only under particular circumstances, such as the combination of poor hydrographic conditions and unusually dense aggregation of farming units or highly intensive practices, that severe impacts on the aquatic environment may occur. These considerations are important when deciding whether or not to establish aquaculture-specific reporting, surveillance or monitoring schemes.

149. Nevertheless, existing and future coastal aquaculture activities will certainly benefit from aquatic pollution monitoring programmes assessing environmental changes in coastal areas and, possibly, river basins. Aquaculture-specific monitoring schemes should, where possible, be integrated in existing coastal water pollution assessment activities. Furthermore, the data derived from aquaculture-specific monitoring may also serve as an aid in improving husbandry practice which in itself can be a means of reducing possible ecological effects without lowering production.

150. General principles and requirements for monitoring and surveillance are outlined in section 5.1.2. Considering the variety of coastal aquaculture practices and the diversity of potential ecological effects involved, it is crucial for any aquaculture-specific monitoring activity that its objectives and purposes are well defined. Data collection for monitoring can lead to large and costly programmes. It is essential that monitoring be carefully planned and that the techniques adopted are statistically sound. Therefore, before starting a monitoring activity, a baseline assessment may be required to clearly establish:

- the correct key parameters to be recorded or monitored;
- the duration and the area to be covered;
- the possible achievements and limitations of the approach chosen;
- the skills and equipments required;
- the costs involved; and

the source for financing the monitoring activity.

151. For monitoring to be an effective means of indicating that ecological change does not exceed a predetermined level it is necessary to identify and where possible quantify the change in a particular parameter. At present, however, there is considerable debate regarding which key parameters should be monitored to assess a given effect (Gowen *et al.*, 1990).

152. The right choice of parameters will be determined by the circumstances encountered, e.g. type of coastal aquaculture practice, production level and the physical and ecological conditions prevailing in the area. A cursory overview of parameters and characteristics for which data may be collected is given in **Annex 4**.

153. It is important that suitable control stations are located. The frequency and timing of sampling have to be related to the nature of the parameters being monitored, and consideration should also be given to effects of natural variation and seasonality in a given parameter. Standardization of both methodology and description of parameters (in terms of units, dimensions, relationships, ratios, rates, etc.) is emphasized.

## 5.3 Role and Functions of Environmental Impact Assessment (EIA)

154. Environmental impact assessment (EIA) will be discussed briefly, as it is sometimes viewed as a management tool or as a regulatory mechanism or a policy instrument. There is no "standard" or "ideal" EIA. EIA is controversial and is still being discussed and improved in terms of scope, objectives and procedures. There are many definitions and concepts of EIA, including different terminologies (Jernelov and Marinov, 1990). Means of practical EIA implementation and features of incorporation of EIA in institutional frameworks of countries and international organizations are very diverse (ERL, 1990). This diversity in EIA is a positive feature, reflecting different circumstances and requirements wherever EIA is to be applied.

### 5.3.1 Purposes of EIA

155. According to UNEP (1988), EIA is a management tool like economic analysis and engineering feasibility studies. EIA (1) predicts the likely environmental impacts of projects, (2) finds ways to reduce unacceptable impacts and to shape the project so as that it suits the local environment, and (3) presents these predictions and options to decision-makers. Bisset (1989) lists the following objectives of EIA:

(a) to identify beneficial and adverse environmental impacts;
(b) to suggest mitigation actions which might reduce or prevent adverse impacts;
(c) to suggest measures which might enhance beneficial impacts;
(d) to identify and describe the residual adverse impacts which cannot be mitigated;
(e) to identify appropriate monitoring strategies to "track" impacts and provide an "early warning" system;
(f) to incorporate environmental information into the decision making process relating to development projects; and,
(g) to aid selection of the "optimum" alternative (if alternative sites or project designs are being investigated in an EIA study).

156. Aspects of "modern" EIA include the understanding of EIA as a positive, improvement-oriented approach and as an iterative process (and not as a single study), whereby consultation and public participation are included and socio-economic and socio-cultural issues are covered (Driver and Bisset, 1989). An overview of socio-economic parameters which may need to be considered in coastal aquaculture development is given in **Annex 5**. Aspects of social monitoring and evaluation in aquaculture projects are reviewed by Molnar and Duncan (1989).

### 5.3.2 The EIA sequence

157. In general, the EIA process would contain three main parts: environmental appraisal, monitoring and evaluation. The environmental appraisal would consist of four key steps: screening, preliminary assessment, scoping and detailed assessment (see also **Figure 15**).

158. In a first step, projects are screened according to pre-determined criteria to decide whether or not further appraisal is required. Criteria on potential significant environmental impact may include type and size of projects, environmental sensitivity of areas, or combination of both. More flexible case-by-case approaches may also be followed.

159. The preliminary assessment step applies to projects which would require further environmental appraisal. Here, a proposed project would be appraised in terms of: likely environmental impact based on initial impact prediction, purpose, societal need, technological requirements and costs, location, level of resource utilization, people and communities potentially affected, alternatives (including technological improvement and adaptation of project), and possible mitigation measures. This step identifies projects with limited environmental implications that can be readily overcome. Provided appropriate adaptation and mitigation measures are identified and incorporated into the project design, no further assessment would be required.

160. Scoping applies to projects which are likely to have serious environmental consequences and which will need thorough examination and assessment. Here, the scope of a detailed EIA is determined in terms of objectives and major issues, appropriate methodology, data requirements, geographical boundaries, time horizon of analysis, costs involved, expertise required, affected groups, institutions, agencies, and possible alternatives.

161. Detailed assessment of proposed projects may require baseline studies on the current and past state of the environment. Assessment and prediction methods are then used to identify impacts and to predict their magnitude. A monitoring programme may be developed and ameliorative/mitigative measures may be formulated.

162. Monitoring provides an early warning that adverse effects (predicted or not) are occurring. Monitoring can be useful for continued generation of EIA inputs to management (e.g., mid-course corrections, effectiveness of and compliance with recommended mitigation measures, and improvement of predictions). All projects which may cause significant negative environmental effects should include a monitoring component. In cases where the environmental appraisal has confirmed that the effects will not be significant, and that adequate steps have been taken to minimize the identified effects, monitoring may consist of periodic reviews of the main areas of concern.

163. Through evaluation of completed projects the accuracy of predictions and the relevance of recommendations are judged against actual experience. Evaluation may help to identify additional significant effects warranting corrective actions. Evaluation results can prove useful to refine impact predictions for future projects of the same type and magnitude.

164. **Figure 16 and Table 14** show when and how an EIA can contribute to the various stages of the project cycle. In order to show the variety in approaches and terminology, examples of other EIA sequences are given in **Annex 6**.

### 5.3.3 Methodologies in EIA

165. There are more than 100 techniques and formats for carrying out EIAs including check-lists, environmental evaluation, matrices, networks, environmental indices, cost-benefit analysis, overlay mapping, simulation modelling workshops, which are reviewed elsewhere (ESCAP, 1985; Shopley and Fuggle, 1984; Carpenter and Maragos, 1989). Often, the resources required to carry out an EIA include: (1) establishment of a qualified multi-disciplinary team and analytical facilities, (2)

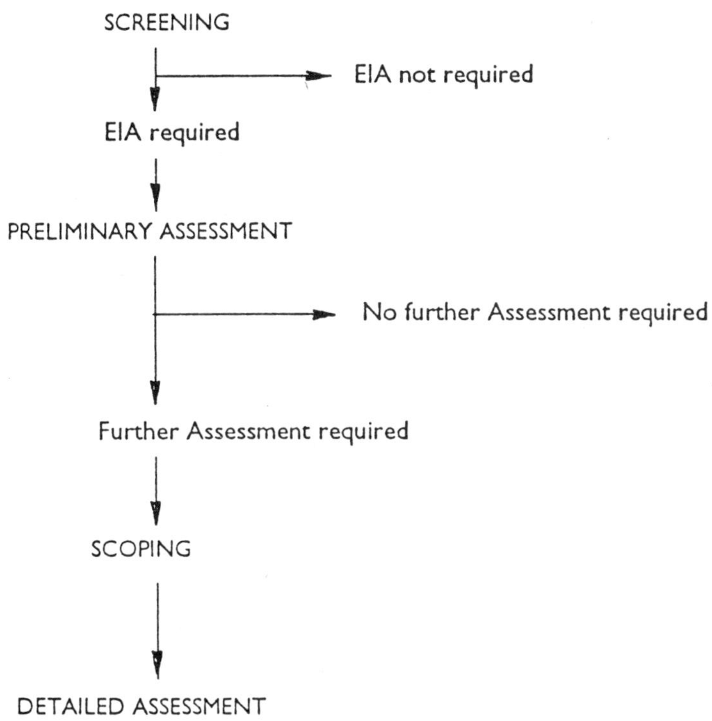


**Figure 15:** The EIA process (from Driver and Bisset, 1989)

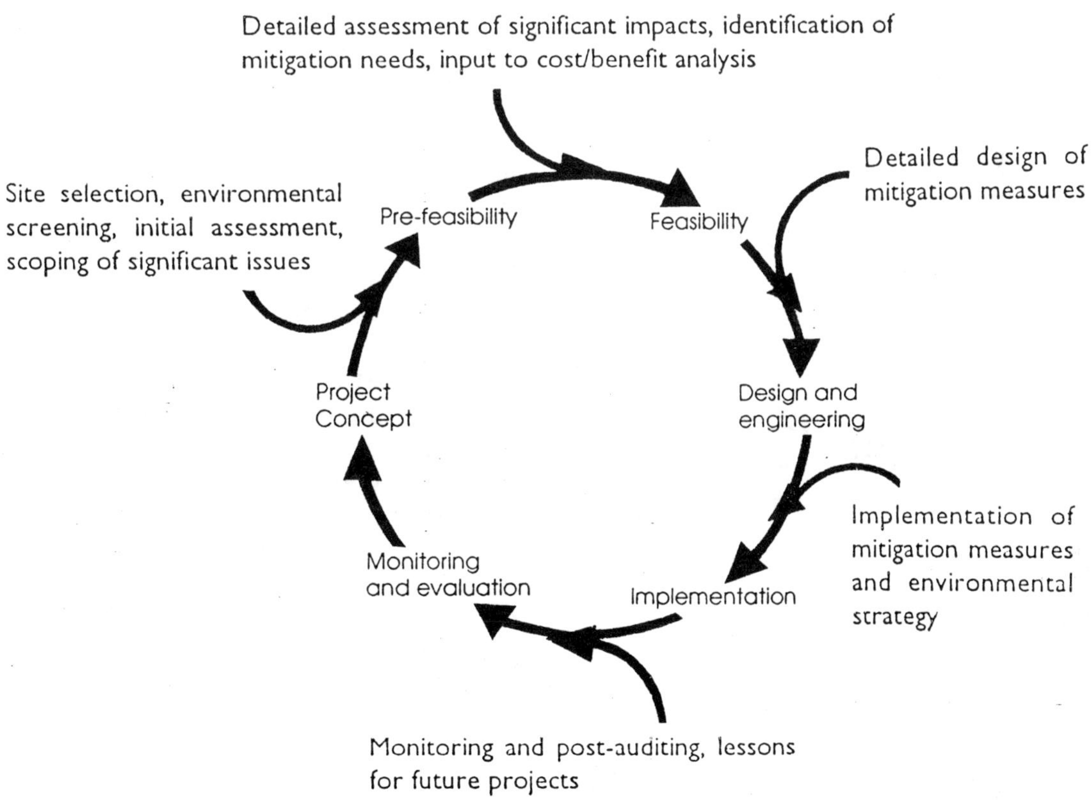


**Figure 16:** EIA and the project cycle (from Driver and Bisset, 1989)

**Table 14**: EIA in the project sequence. Note: the exact correspondence varies among projects (from Carpenter and Maragos, 1989).

| Stage of the project | EIA process |
|---|---|
| 1. Conception | • Screening for obvious environmental problems based on previous experience |
| | • Scoping of significant issues for possible EIA |
| 2. Prefeasibility | • Review of site for ecological sensitivities |
| | • Application of findings of generic EIA for the technologies intended |
| | • Initial assessment |
| | • Gathering of baseline environmental data |
| | • Public participation in project planning |
| 3. Feasibility | • Prediction and quantification of impacts |
| | • Review of EIA by public and independent experts |
| | • Interaction with engineering analysis for proposing alternative technologies |
| | • Identification of needed prevention and mitigation measures |
| | • Valuation of externalities |
| | • Benefit-cost analysis |
| | • Negotiation of environmental protection covenants in financing agreements |
| 4. Design and engineering | • Detailed design of mitigation measures, refinement of impact predictions, and economic analyses including cost effectiveness |
| | • Monitoring programme designed |
| 5. Implementation | • Installation of mitigation measures |
| | • Mid-course correction based on actual performance |
| 6. Operation and maintenance | • Monitoring for compliance and testing for accuracy of predictions |
| 7. Completed project evaluation | • Post-audit and lessons learned for future EIAs |

access to EIA techniques, (3) financial and institutional support, and (4) monitoring and enforcement powers.

### 5.3.4 Problems and limitations in EIA

166. In many countries, an inadequate database and lack of trained personnel are likely to be major constraints. Implementation of EIA in many countries faces problems due to:

- poor availability and reliability of data;
- insufficient training/education in EIA methodologies and in the establishment of appropriate legal and regulatory frameworks and institutional arrangements;
- negligence of beneficial impacts in EIA reports;
- lack of consideration of alternative sites, technologies, designs, and strategies;
- insufficient involvement and participation of all interested and affected parties;
- insufficient emphasis on required cost-effectiveness of EIA;
- lateness in implementation and lack of follow-up monitoring and evaluation;
- inappropriate recommendations, e.g., mitigation/adaptation measures which are not affordable or feasible in terms of maintenance requirements or operating costs;
- poor presentation of EIA results.

167. Also, scientific knowledge about ecological cause-effect relationships and modelling of ecosystems is still developing which limits the capacity to quantitatively predict all environmental changes. Similarly, techniques for economic valuation of environmental impacts also need to be improved although much progress in identifying and including so-called offsite and future externalities has been made (see for example Dixon, 1989; Bergstrom, 1991; Dixon *et al.*, 1986; Hufschmidt *et al.*, 1983; Dixon and Hufschmidt, 1986; Klaassen and Opschoor, 1991; Pierce, 1988).

### 5.3.5 Alternatives to EIA

168. Although the implementation of EIA and its integration in regulatory and institutional frameworks probably contribute to the process of sustainable development, alternatives to EIA, which are more suited to the database in the countries concerned and to their levels of personnel and other resources should also be explored and emphasized. Of particular importance in this context are physical planning procedures and rules for land zoning and land use.

169. For example, land planning may have to intervene in the functioning of markets when the existence of externalities or public good result in market outcomes that are unfavourable to sustainable resource use. From the standpoint of legal instruments, this involves, *inter alia*, the resolution of competing demands for land in relation to the predetermined development goals, criteria and priorities (FAO/Netherlands, 1991b).

170. Generally, there is an increasing trend to combine approaches and methodologies to resolve environmental and socio-economic development issues, which is reflected, for example, in recent guidelines for land-use planning, rural-area development planning and economic-cum-environmental development planning (FAO, 1989b, 1991b; Bendavid-Val, 1990; ADB, 1991a, 1991b, 1988). Recently, the United Nations Development Programme also produced a handbook and guidelines for environmental management and sustainable development (UNDP, 1991).

## 6. OPTIONS FOR ENVIRONMENTAL MANAGEMENT OF COASTAL AQUACULTURE DEVELOPMENT

171. In this section, a number of environmental management options are presented, many of which are already being implemented. First, a general management framework for protection of coastal environments is described (6.1). An overview on the integrated coastal area management approach is given (6.2) and legislation governing coastal aquaculture is discussed (6.3). The role and functions of planning and management of coastal aquaculture development are addressed (6.4) and environmental management options at farm or project level are summarized (6.5). It is emphasized that these management options reflect approaches which are - to some extent - conceptually different.

172. Circumstances at local, district and central government levels will have to be considered in the choice and the implementation of these management options, possibly involving a selection or combination of relevant elements of these options. This choice should be based on a proper understanding of the interactions between aquaculture and the environment as well as adequate knowledge of environmental impact assessment methods and procedures.

### 6.1 A Management Framework for Protection of Coastal Environments

173. A management framework for protection of coastal environments follows, adapted from GESAMP (1991b). Environmental impact assessment efforts should be guided by predetermined development priorities and well-formulated environmental protection objectives. It is equally important that, based on environmental impact assessment, the environmental performance of coastal activities is monitored and controlled according to well-defined directives and regulations specific to those activities which pose a significant threat to the coastal environment.

174. GESAMP's environmental management framework has three components: the management planning process, the environmental impact assessment process and the regulatory process (see Figure 17). Ten action levels are specified in relation to important considerations and factors. This framework and the management processes it describes are continuous institutional functions and not functions that are triggered only by individual development proposals.

175. Within the management planning process both overall and specific goals (developmental benefits and desired environmental conditions) are adopted, and values and resource uses identified and prioritized. At action level (3) the task is to determine the environmental characteristics that sustain specified values and resources, and the extent to which these can be changed without causing harm.

176. These limiting values are normally expressed as environmental quality criteria that can be used to formulate site-and contaminant-specific standards. As stated before, due consideration should hereby be given to size/intensity of the waste-generating activity and the environmental capacity of receiving waterbodies. Fish consumption patterns should be reflected in contaminant levels established for edible species.

177. The environmental impact assessment process includes action levels (4) and (5) where the current environmental situation is assessed, and existing and potential inputs are identified and quantified. At level (6) current and projected resource uses are appraised in view of the environmental capacities determined. If necessary, means to reduce effects are formulated which should also include adaptation and modification of resource utilization. In the case that environmental capacity is exceeded, envisaged development will have to be reassessed. If required, all feasible mitigation and control options are compared at level (7) to select those that are most useful and efficient in meeting specific goals and priorities.

178. Within the regulatory process, operational and corrective action is taken at level (8),

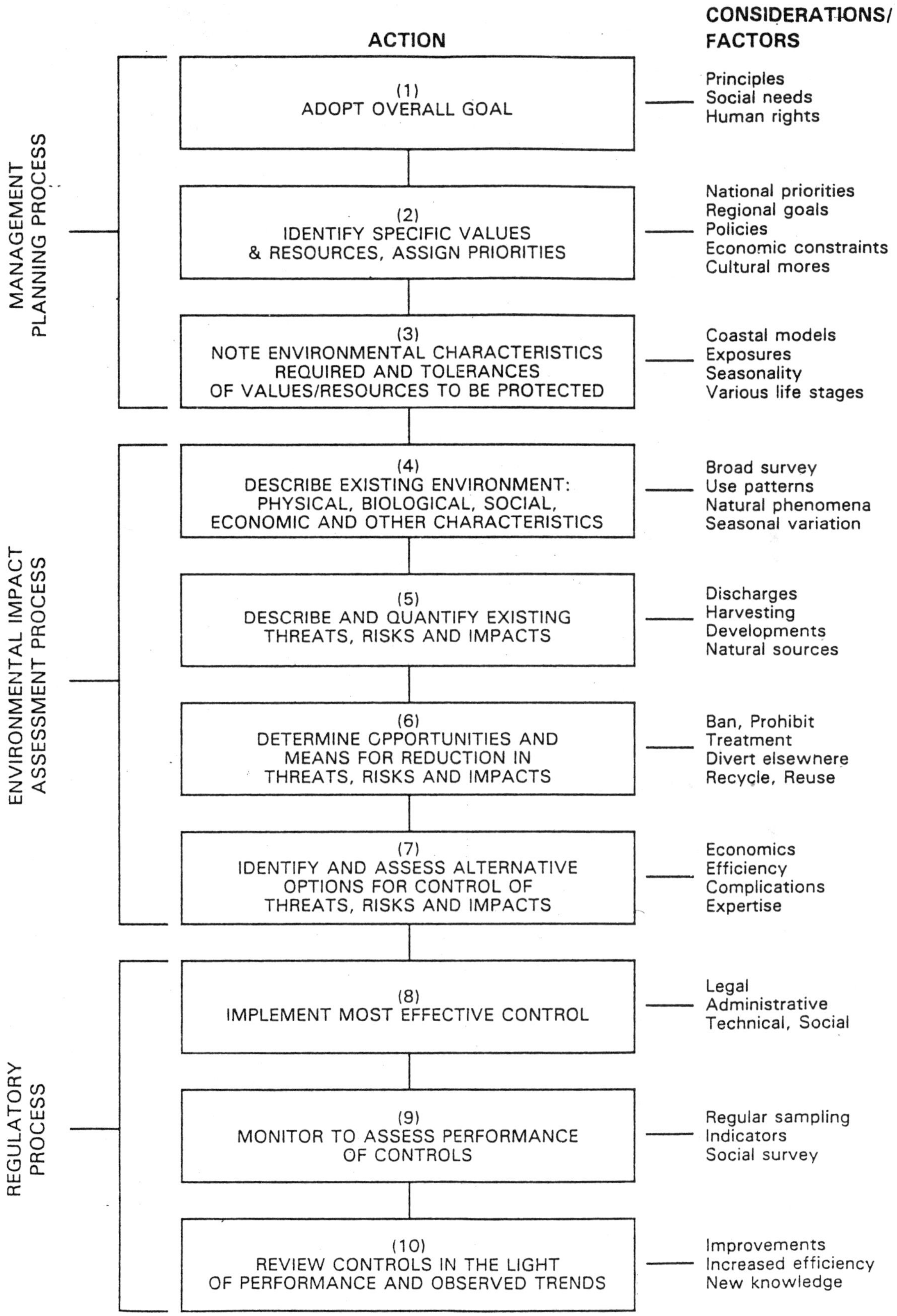


**Figure 17**: Comprehensive management framework for protection of marine and other environments (from GESAMP, 1991b)

whereby required controls are applied to activities carrying environmental risks as identified at level (5). Regulatory measures could range from imposed limits on the chemical concentrations in effluents, to the temporary banning of certain products and practices. They could also involve financial incentives or disincentives, subsidies, fines, imposed waste treatment or public awareness campaigns including consumer education. The effectiveness of control measures is measured - in level (9) - through monitoring programmes: first, to ensure compliance with controls imposed on certain activities, and second, to regularly measure those variables that are being used to indicate that specific goals are being achieved. Finally, there needs to be a commitment to act if the monitoring programme indicates either that there is a lack of compliance with controls, or that they are ineffective, or a trend indicates that limiting criteria are in danger of being approached. Such action - level (10) - following monitoring completes the management loop.

*Basic prerequisites for implementation of GESAMP's management framework*

179. With regard to implementation of these management processes, GESAMP emphasizes the following requirements:

180. **Environmental planning**: There is a requirement for coordinated multi-sectoral planning of developments that have the potential to affect the marine environment. This should include the assignment of environmental goals and priorities, resource allocations, and the preparation of integrated management plans for all relevant sectors.

181. **Environmental impact assessments**: All proposed large-scale developments and investments that are likely to have direct or indirect effects on the marine environment must be subject to a prior assessment. This assessment should encompass physical, chemical and biological changes, risks to human health, amenities and resources and, particularly, the benefits and detriments of the proposal to the satisfaction of environmental and development goals.

182. **The need for precaution**: Precaution is integral to scientific risk assessment. A pessimistic approach is essential to allow for uncertainties in measurements and calculations incorporated into predictions. Science should be used to resolve and reduce these uncertainties by providing accurate information on the relationship between the practice and its effect on marine resources. A further, and entirely complementary, use of precaution is to take all practical and economically feasible measures to minimize environmental contamination through *inter alia* good housekeeping and the application of efficient and low-waste technologies.

183. **Acceptance of change**: Implicit in this framework is an acceptance that change is both a feature of the natural environment and an inevitable consequence of human activities and social development. Human intervention to limit and control such changes is both necessary and legitimate.

*Basic criteria for adapting an environmental management framework to coastal aquaculture*

184. The following basic criteria may also prove useful in formulating, establishing and improving the institutional and regulatory framework for environmental management of coastal aquaculture (adapted from Muir and Baird, 1991). The environmental management system should be characterized by:

185. **Simplicity**: It should be as easy as possible to operate, and be clear and understandable to all those involved, including the public.

186. **Equity**: It should operate fairly on all those involved in 'using' coastal resources, according to the degree of use. This should extend to apply to all users, as well as aquaculturists.

187. **Capacity**: Implementing institutions may require strengthening through training and equipment; however, due account should be given to actual requirements and financial resources

available.

188. **Fair distribution of costs:** The system should not be too burdensome, and either overload or excessively inhibit the activities it is designed to cover, or place too great an imposition on the institutions responsible for its operation.

189. **Rationality:** It should be based on logical and scientific foundations, providing testability and, once operational, offering predictive power.

## 6.2 Integrated Coastal Area Management (ICAM)

190. Coastal aquaculture is one of many activities utilizing coastal resources. The lack of appropriate cross-sectoral coordination and control of development of the various coastal activities has, to some extent, contributed to natural resources depletion, environmental degradation and resource-use conflicts. In many cases, it may be required that coastal aquaculture is developed within the overall framework of a coastal area planning and management programme. A brief overview on ICAM follows, which may prove useful for coastal aquaculture development planners.

191. There is a variety of approaches and concepts to coastal management. Sorensen and McCreary (1990) list and review 11 strategies for management of coastal resources and environments, including national economic planning, broad-scope sectoral planning of coastal uses or resources, regional seas, nation- or state-wide land-use planning and regulation, special area or regional plans, shoreland exclusion or restriction, environmental impact assessment of coastal development proposals, mandatory policies and advisory guidelines, acquisition programmes, coastal atlases and databanks.

### 6.2.1 Definitions and concepts related to ICAM

192. The coastal area is an interface between the land and the sea which extends inland and seaward to a variable extent. The term "coastal area" refers to a geographic space which has not been defined as a zone. Defining boundaries of a "coastal zone" in a given area ("zoning") will depend on political, administrative, ecological and pragmatic considerations. For example, where there is a broad array of possible coastal issues and impacts the boundaries may be taken as those of the area with highest intensity of conflictual use. If watershed issues are of concern, then an inland extension of the "coastal management zone" is necessary. Zoning, i.e., the process of defining the boundaries of a coastal area to be developed and managed, is an essential component of ICAM.

193. ICAM is both a concept and a tool for inter-sectoral coordination. It incorporates modern principles of decision-making in planning and natural resources areal management, interdisciplinary processes, intensive information bases. It is foreseen as an effective general framework for dealing with the interactions of the various uses of the coastal areas, based on consultation and participation of resource users and managers. ICAM aims at a balance between a variety of compatible uses whereby economic and social benefits are maximized and conservation and development become compatible goals. Integration hereby refers to (1) the various sectors (e.g., fisheries, waste disposal, marine transport), (2) to the tasks of which ICAM is comprised and (3) to the economic, technological, ecological, and institutional aspects involved.

194. ICAM is typically concerned with resolving conflicts among the many uses of coastal resources and trying to determine the optimal mix of uses over time, recognizing the dynamic nature of both resources and demands on those resources. An ICAM programme usually has the following attributes:

It is implemented by government in response to very evident resource degradation, hazard exposure, and multiple-use conflicts, or as part of planning for regional or national economic development.

- As a programme it is ongoing and therefore distinct from a one-time project. It has longevity and is usually a response to a legislative or executive mandate.

- The programme relates to a physical area with landward and seaward limits defined as the coastal zone.

- It addresses a specific set of objectives or issues. These issues, and/or the relative importance among issues, are likely to change over time.

- The programme has an institutional identity, i.e. it is identifiable as either an independent organization or (more often) as a cooperating network of organizations linked to by formal mechanisms which allocate tasks among the organizations (entities, agencies).

### 6.2.2 Programme formulation

195. Objectives and priorities as well as content and complexity of an ICAM programme will vary from area to area according to development trends, conservation needs, traditions, norms, governmental systems, and current critical issues and conflicts. But compatible multiple-use objectives should always be the main focus. If human and financial resources are limited, ICAM programmes can be simplified to include only the following components (FAO, 1991c): (i) harmonization of sectoral policies and goals; (ii) cross-sectoral enforcement mechanisms; (iii) a coordination office and (iv) permit approval and environmental impact assessment (EIA) procedures.

196. According to FAO (1991c) ICAM programmes should relate to national planning and possibly to specific coastal development plans. They should provide advice to developers and managers, coordinate agencies and stakeholders towards agreed goals. They should provide opportunities for analyses of options, of legislation and institutions and for the creation of an information base. Some considerations which may guide the formulation of ICAM programmes are provided in **Annex 7**. An example for the development of an ICAM plan (Chua 1989) is given in **Figure 18**. Chua (1991) summarized processes in identifying ICAM issues and formulating ICAM plans (see **Figure 19**).

197. ICAM planning should start with a "strategy plan" that lays the foundation for the legislation or the executive order that is needed to authorize the programme development stage that follows. The strategy plan should (FAO, 1991c):

- state clearly the objectives of the ICAM programme;

- indicate how theses objectives will be met;

- assign responsibility for the programme to a particular agency;

- identify the funding necessary for programme development;

- ensure collaboration among the various sectoral agencies and private interests involved;

- state the time limits involved for various stages of programme development.

### 6.2.3 The information base

198. Information needs for ICAM planning should be determined in a preliminary analysis of the given situation, based primarily on existing data (Clark, 1991), aimed at:

(a) estimating the levels and spatial patterns of coastal activities, at present, and for target

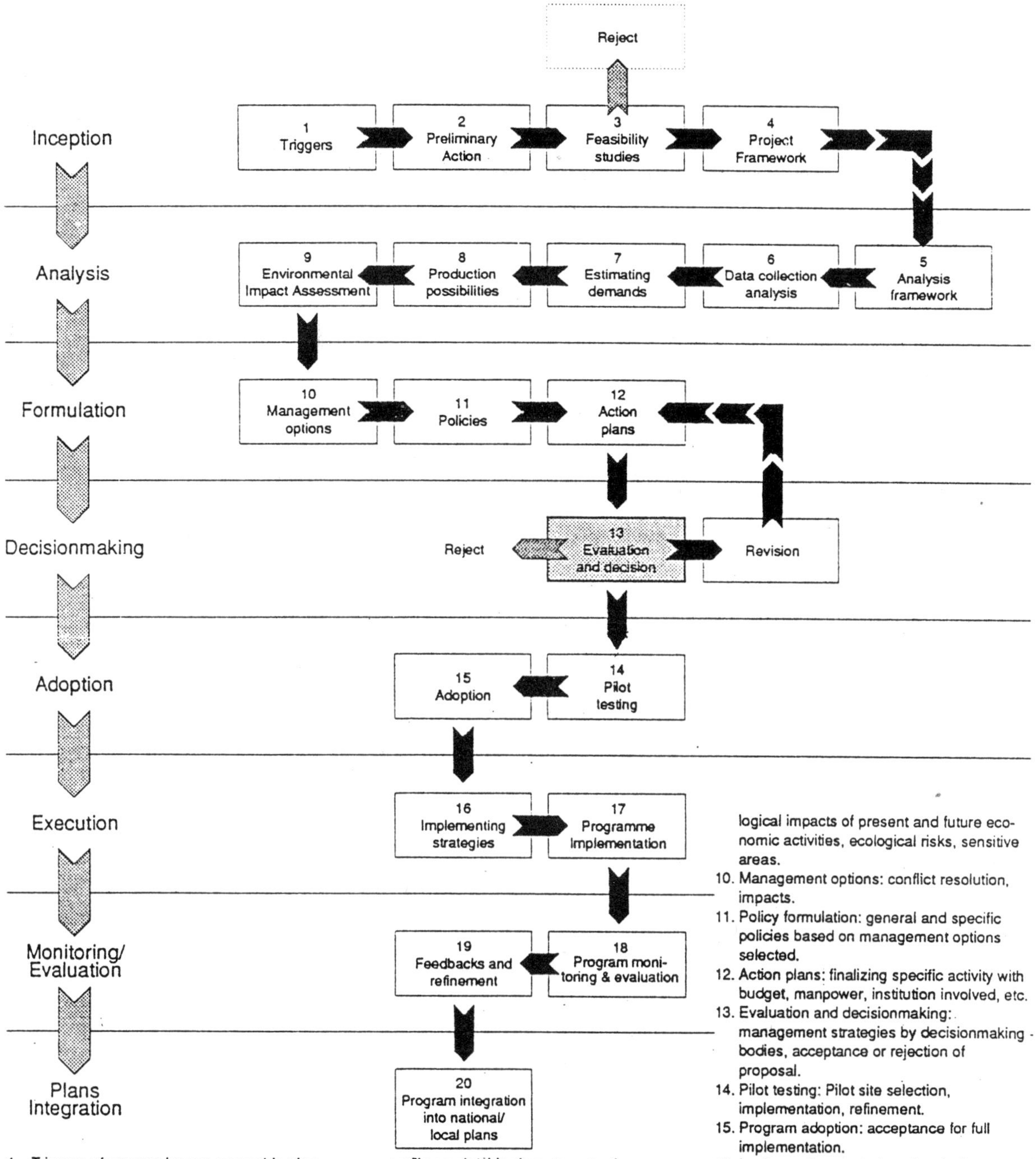


1. Triggers of process by one or combination of factors: a. resource depletion; b. pollution; c. environment incident; d. concern for sustainable development; e. other factors.
2. Preliminary action: awareness of coastal issues and initiation of formal process.
3. Feasibility study: assessment of coastal issues, management needs.
4. Setting up the project framework: project formulation, determining coordination institution, project document.
5. Setting up the analysis framework: coastal profile, goals/objectives, targets, time frame, boundaries, approaches/scenarios, criteria for evaluation/monitoring, legal/ institutional framework.
6. Carrying out analysis: issues, causes, impacts, constraints.
7. Estimating demands for products/services; types of products and services generated; demand level.
8. Analysing production possibilities: output estimate, strategies, attainments.
9. Environmental Impact Assessment: ecological impacts of present and future economic activities, ecological risks, sensitive areas.
10. Management options: conflict resolution, impacts.
11. Policy formulation: general and specific policies based on management options selected.
12. Action plans: finalizing specific activity with budget, manpower, institution involved, etc.
13. Evaluation and decisionmaking: management strategies by decisionmaking bodies, acceptance or rejection of proposal.
14. Pilot testing: Pilot site selection, implementation, refinement.
15. Program adoption: acceptance for full implementation.
16. Implementing strategies: developing various strategies for action plan implementation.
17. Program implementation: implementing institution, carry out action.
18. Program monitoring/evaluation: assessing attainment of objectives and impacts.
19. Feedback and refinement: setting up feedback mechanism, refinement needed.
20. Plan integration: integrating CAMP national/local government development plans.

**Figure 18:** An example for the development of an integrated coastal area management plan (from Chua, 1989)

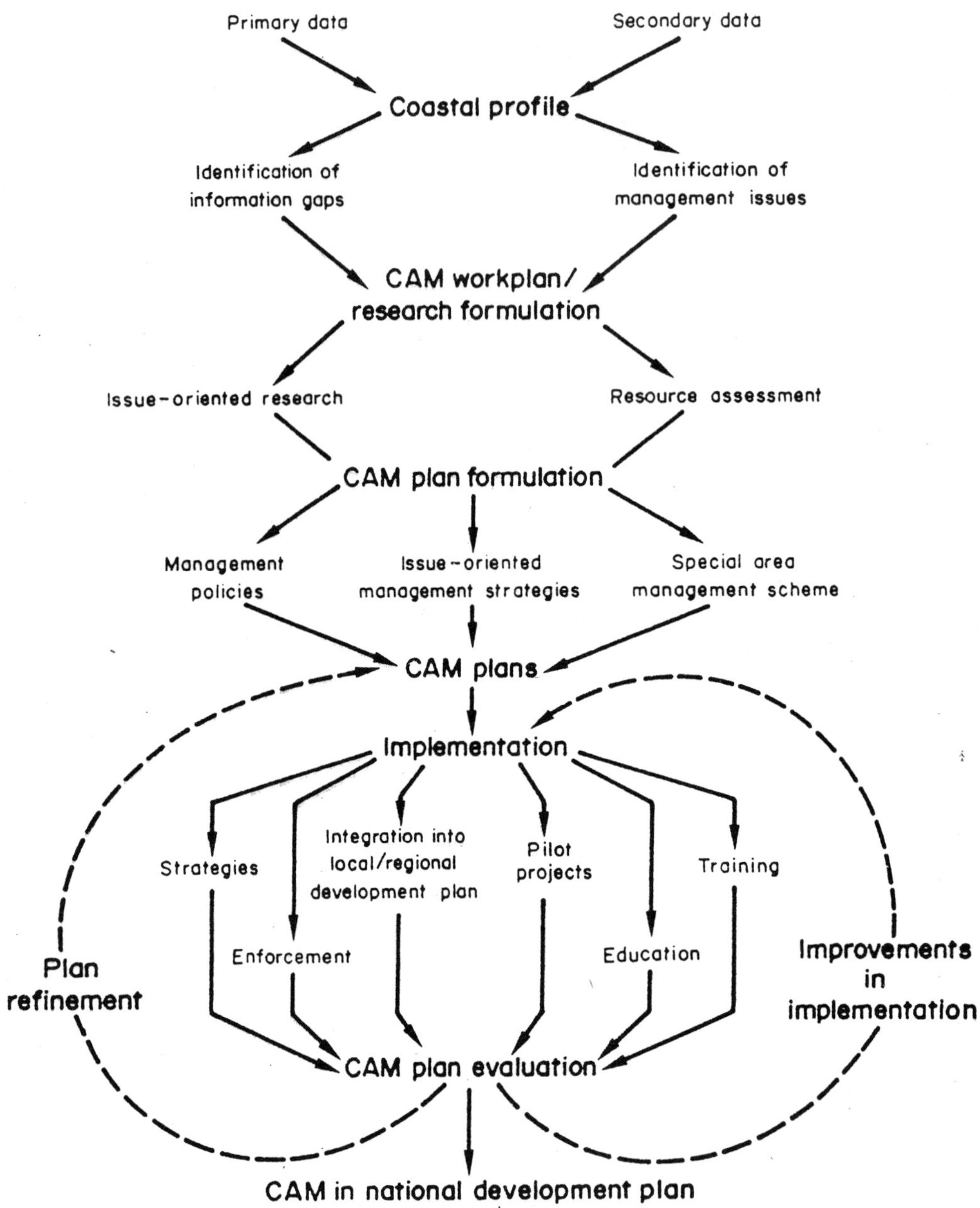


Figure 19: Processes in identifying coastal area management issues and formulating coastal area management plans (from Chua, 1991)

years in the future;

(b) estimating demands for use of coastal resources as a result of the activities in (a);

(c) analysing possible means for producing/satisfying the demands estimated in (b);

(d) analysing the impacts of the activities on coastal ecosystems, based on both waste discharge to the coast and on space occupancy of coastal areas;

(e) formulating and evaluating strategies for ICAM (a strategy being comprised of a mix of outputs, physical measures, operating procedures, implementation incentives, institutional arrangements, and financing programme);

(f) presenting the results to decision-makers and interested parties.

199. Some principal types of information needed for ICAM are given in **Annex 8**. Inventories, atlases, databases related to resources, habitats, environments and present or potential development activities are considered very useful in ICAM. Particularly useful are geographical information systems (GIS) which assist in retrieving, compiling and using existing but not easily available information on resources, environments and uses (Meaden and Kapetsky, 1991; Cendrero, 1989a; Kam, 1989; FAO, 1989a; Butler *et al.,* 1988; Kapetsky *et al.,* 1987; FAO, 1985b). These also help to identify data gaps, reducing the need for additional information to a minimum. For examples on the collection of ICAM information, the reader is referred to coastal environmental profiles which have been elaborated for several areas in Southeast Asia (McManus and Chua, 1990; White, Martosubroto and Sadorra, 1989; Chia, Habibullah and Chou, 1988; Paw *et al.,* 1988; Chua *et al.,* 1987).

### 6.2.4 Management strategies

200. Management may be reactive or proactive. Reactive integrated management is an issue-driven process and the nature of the particular issues dictates the type of programme to be created and the boundaries of the programme. In this mode, the effort and expense required to set up an ICAM programme would not be justified unless there were multiple issues of importance to be addressed. However, when there is a conflict between different interests, corrective measures might be very difficult to apply. Proactive integrated management is part of the development planning. It may help to avoid the most serious conflicts by making the "right" decisions early in the process. This consideration is particularly important for developing countries. Some premises and considerations for a management strategy in ICAM are given in **Annex 9**.

201. Several specific management strategies have been used as elements of integrated coastal resources management programmes (Clark, 1991; Lowry, 1989):

202. Through zoning schemes, space and resources are allocated, explicitly and legally, to different types of uses which may include nature and biodiversity conservation.

203. Protected areas (and biosphere reserves) may provide custodial protection for critical or particularly sensitive areas and species. However, protected areas may also be coupled with multiple use zones; an approach which would include a strictly protected "core area" linked with adjacent buffering areas and multiple use zones. This combination is less likely to result in strong resistance than undifferentiated reserves.

204. Shoreline exclusion zones are designed to specifically prohibit or significantly limit uses within a strip or band in the coastal zone. The shoreline exclusion zone is primarily used to ensure public access, preserve the landscape and protect shore areas from erosion. The areas subject to shoreland restriction are typically landward to the high water mark.

205. Specific zones may be designated to priority activities. The priority activity in a particular zone may acquire "predominant use" status. Other "permitted uses" can be accommodated, but only as long as they do not jeopardize the predominant use. Zoning designations are usually designed to anticipate and coordinate future uses rather than respond to specific development proposals, as do permit systems.

206. In the typical permit system, specific coastal uses within a specified coastal zone are subject to authorization. Applications for permits usually require information about the intended activity and the nature of impacts likely to be generated by the activity (see sections on assessment of environmental impacts).

207. Facility-siting guidelines are special requirements for particular projects likely to have major coastal impacts. Some facility guidelines specify a particular review process with which a project must comply. Others specify standards with regard to emissions and effluents that a facility must meet (see sections on assessment of environmental impacts).

208. Establishment of ownership and tenure systems may be the most certain way to protect and manage critical habitats and their resources. If the areas are owned by the state, access may have to be restricted and controlled to avoid degradation due to competition. Exclusive user rights may be given for certain types of resources or areas, to coastal communities or to private interests. The devolution of user rights and management responsibilities to coastal communities may help to promote cost-effective coastal management. The use of financial incentives or disincentives may also help to control extraction or pollution rates.

209. Communication and negotiation patterns between parties involved in ICAM may need to be improved (see Lowry, 1989). Facilitated policy dialogues deal with policy conflicts at the planning stage. A neutral facilitator organizes meetings to resolve inter-agency or other conflicts. The facilitator helps the group structure an agenda and guides discussions in an orderly fashion. Mediation is important in multiparty resource-use or site-use disputes. This involves the use of a non-partisan party who designs a process which ensures that all relevant parties are represented and identify their interests; and who makes it possible for disputants to present options that deal with the interests of each party and to draw up agreements.

### 6.2.5 Implementation and enforcement

210. Experience in ICAM is limited because the integration of coastal areas development and management is a relatively new concept. Experiences in the planning and implementation of ICAM made so far in developing and industrialized countries are very diverse (Clark, 1991; Burbridge, 1991; Chua and Scura, 1991; Sorensen and McCreary, 1990; Chua and Pauly, 1989; Juhasz, 1991; Bashirullah *et al.*, 1989; Merschrod, 1989; Chen, 1989; Katz, 1989; Kennedy, 1990; Chong and Manwan, 1987; Charlier, 1989: Cendrero, 1989b; Archer, 1988; Hildebrand, 1989; Gubbay, 1990). Coastal area management approaches specifically designed for coastal aquaculture in industrialized countries also exist (see for example Black, in press; Pedersen *et al.*, 1988).

211. There are many ICAM-related strategies, policies and plans produced by experts governments and international organizations. However, implementation of ICAM programmes has often faced serious difficulties and constraints which led to poor achievement of ICAM objectives.

212. Main difficulties and reasons for failures of ICAM programmes include: lack of technical and financial support; lack of long-term political commitment; issues of common property resources and allocation of resource user rights; lack of people's awareness, motivation and participation; inadequate institutions and administrative fragmentation; inadequate definition of coastal zone boundaries; lack of clearly stated goals; lack of compatibility with sectoral development plans; dominance of "crisis" management over long-range planning and proactive management; inadequate information bases and research capacity; lack of trained personnel; difficulty to identify the competent counterpart agency.

213. Financial constraints are a particularly serious matter, especially for developing countries. Sources of funds for ICAM need to be identified which may include licences and user fees and taxes under the "polluter pays" and "user pays" principles, international grants and softloans, percentage on development programmes, etc.

214. Some level of enforcement is required in all management programmes. This presumes the existence of an operational legal framework and entails costs. Enforcement costs depend on the level of people's adhesion and cooperation as well as on the system of regulatory control measures, incentives and disincentives adopted. Right-based systems appear to be cheaper to enforce as they can rely more on self-enforcement.

## 6.3 Legislation Governing Coastal Aquaculture

215. Legislative and administrative measures aiming at the environmental compatibility of the various aquaculture practices should be considered within the broader legislative context governing coastal aquaculture. Many countries have little or no aquaculture-specific legislation purposely designed to protect or allow this activity. However, many aquaculturists must cope with complex laws and regulations on land tenure, water use, environment protection, pollution prevention, public health and fisheries in general. Few of these are specifically drafted to promote or regulate aquaculture, and confusion, conflicts and overlapping exist (Van Houtte *et al.*, 1989).

216. A particular legal regime for coastal aquaculture in an individual country must ensure that the needs of aquaculturists are met, but also that existing or future relevant laws are carefully integrated. Purpose and scope of legislative measures should be well defined. Legislation should clearly take into consideration:

(a) the purposes of the industry: e.g., food production and market (local or export), employment, recreation, etc.;
(b) the resources or species used;
(c) the system or elements utilized for production; and
(d) the environment in which production is conducted.

217. Various preventive and remedial measures for controlling and managing the environmental impact of aquaculture have been developed and applied (see for example Van Houtte *et al.*, 1989; Bye, 1990; Quincy, 1990; McCoy, 1989; Howarth, 1990; Rosenthal *et al.*, 1988). A summary of control options used in various industrialized countries is given in **Table 15**. Van Houtte *et al.* (1989) identified five regulatory approaches, including (i) land use planning and zoning, (ii) control over installation and operation, (iii) discharge limits and pre-discharge treatment to meet limits, (iv) fiscal incentives, and (v) prohibitions.

218. When planning the use of land and water resources the zoning of areas for aquaculture purposes should be included. Also, once protected areas such as parks and nature reserves are established, it should be clearly stated where and under which conditions aquaculture practices would be permitted, if at all. Aquaculture practices should not be permitted in heavily polluted waters. Pollution hazards to aquaculture and its produce should be properly assessed in high-risk areas.

219. Environmental impact assessments (EIA) or environmental impact statements (EIS) on the potential effects of proposed large-scale aquaculture operations may be imposed prior to the authorization for the installation of an aquafarm. In the former, the investor is usually required to make a general statement of the effects of the project on the environment; in the latter the statement is much more rigorous and may require all facts about the project and a detailed estimate of its effects on the environment.

220. Specific coastal aquaculture activities/installations may be termed and classified as

**Table 15:** A summary of aquaculture control options used in various industrialized countries (from NCC, 1989)

| Control option | Canada | Denmark | Finland | France | Japan | New Zealand | Norway | Sweden | USA |
|---|---|---|---|---|---|---|---|---|---|
| Substantial legislation | | | | | | | | | + |
| Distance limits | | | | | | | | | |
| - between sites | | | | + | | | + | | |
| - from conservation areas | + | | | | | | | | |
| Limits on production | | | | | | | | | |
| - per farm | + | | + | | | | | | |
| - cage area or number | + | | | | + | | | | + |
| - by volume | | | | | | | + | | |
| - by stocking density | | | | | + | | | | |
| Water depth regulations | | | | | | + | | | + |
| Restricted areas | | | | | | | + | | |
| Moratorium on new farms | | + | | | | | + | | |
| Regulations on ownership | | | | | | | + | | |
| Environmental Impact Statement (EIS) required | | | | | | | | | + |
| Water quality monitoring | | | + | | | | | | + |
| Management plan required | | | | + | | | | | |
| Regulations vary with farm size | | | + | | | | | + | + |

environmentally critical undertakings, being subject to special declaration or authorization procedures.

221. The installation of effluent quality control equipment or water discharge treatment facilities may be promoted through fiscal incentives like direct subsidies or tax deductions and exemptions. Charges or taxes on polluting effluents also exist.

222. The release of pollutants into adjacent waters through aquaculture or other industries may be regulated by setting quantitative and qualitative limits to the waste waters discharged. Also, in order to meet these limits, the treatment of effluents prior to discharge is often required.

223. Legislation should be enacted to regulate and control the movement of eggs, larvae/juveniles and adult stages of exotic fish species, which may be combined with compulsory certification of stocks to be free of certain diseases and banning of all movements of diseased stocks. Adoption and application of the EIFAC/ICES Codes of Practice on introductions and transfers of marine and freshwater organisms is recommended (Turner, 1988; Arthur and Shariff, 1991; Shariff and Subasinghe, 1990).

224. Coastal aquaculture products should conform with safety standards for seafood before they are allowed for human consumption (see, for example, WHO Expert Committee, 1974). The FAO/WHO Codex Alimentarius Commission is currently preparing a draft code of hygienic practice for the products of aquaculture (FAO/WHO, 1991a), which includes most parts of a draft code of practice for the use of veterinary drugs in aquaculture (FAO/WHO, 1991b). GESAMP (1991c) proposed a code of practice for the use of inhibitory compounds in aquaculture, which is given in **Annex 10**.

225. Constructive and adaptive regulations are needed in order to avoid obstacles to coastal aquaculture development and, equally, to ensure that the environment is adequately protected. Apparent over-regulation and legal uncertainties can, however, hamper aquaculture development, by creating significant barriers to the establishment or the continued operation of aquafarms. It is emphasized that the particular role of aquaculture in utilizing land and water resources for food production calls for an integrative and flexible environmental legislation which is enforceable, effective and adapted to the socio-economic conditions and development needs in local communities, particularly as prevailing in developing countries.

## 6.4 Planning and Management of Coastal Aquaculture Development

226. National aquaculture development plans are always useful not only for identifying where in the country aquaculture should be developed, how this development should take place and the time frame and the resources required. They are also useful for regulating such activities to ensure better chances of success and to minimize developmental and environmental conflicts.

*Past experiences*

227. It has been stated that most aquaculture activities have been developed through isolated and uncoordinated efforts (Pillay, 1990). The growth of aquaculture in the Asian region has generally not been guided by relevant national development plans nor has the industry been adequately managed (Chua and Tech, 1990). Obviously, growth of aquaculture was and is still being driven by market forces. Most private sector-backed development follows these market forces wherein profitability determines the rate of expansion. Comparatively high profit margins have, for example, encouraged the large-scale development of shrimp farming, which, however, is now facing increased international market competition, resulting in considerable price and demand fluctuations and marketability problems. Unfortunately, too much concentration is often given to short-term profits and insufficient attention to long-range planning (see, for example, Hwang, 1992).

228. As for Asia, Chua and Tech (1990) also state that there was no effort to study the opportunities for aquaculture development and their social and environmental implications in the transfer of aquaculture technology from one country to another. This factor was considered to play a part in the failure of many aquaculture projects in Asia.

229. It has also been suggested (UNDP/Norway/FAO, 1987) that international efforts to assist countries in the preparation of national aquaculture development plans proved to be problematical due to: (i) a preoccupation with what is technically possible rather than with what is economically feasible and socially acceptable, (ii) too few and isolated efforts in plan preparation, and (iii) insufficient linkage with a national aquaculture policy. It was further stated that international assistance in the formulation of national aquaculture policies could have been possibly more effective if the assistance had been extended over a longer term and there had been access to decision-makers at a level higher than those responsible for aquaculture or fisheries.

*Towards a more sustainable development of coastal aquaculture*

230. Preliminary guidelines and strategies on improved planning and management of aquaculture development are available (see, for example, Maine and Nash, 1987; ADCP, 1989; Pillay, 1990). Many countries continue efforts to enhance their capacity for planning and management of the aquaculture sector. It is, however, emphasized here that sectoral development efforts be guided by the principle of sustainable development, which is defined by FAO (1988) as:

> *"Sustainable development is the management and conservation of the natural resource base and the orientation of technological and institutional change in such a manner as to ensure the attainment and continued satisfaction of human needs for present and future generations. Such sustainable development (in the agriculture, forestry and fisheries sectors) conserves land, water, plant and animal genetic resources, is environmentally non-degrading, technically appropriate, economically viable and socially acceptable."*

### 6.4.1 Coastal aquaculture in national economic development

231. In many countries, the success of coastal aquaculture development will depend on the degree of prioritization and integration in national plans for economic and agricultural development. Likewise, the success of coastal aquaculture development plans will be determined by the degree of compatibility with development plans for other sectors. Taking the aquaculture practices as relevant for the achievement of sustainable agriculture and rural development (SARD), the following elements of a sustainability strategy are presented as identified by the FAO/Netherlands Conference on Agriculture and the Environment (FAO/Netherlands, 1991a):

(a) **Creating the appropriate policy framework.** Two important objectives should be aimed at:

- widening people's options so that they do not need to harm their environment;
- creating the conditions for market forces to operate efficiently, while providing for corrective measures in cases where the market cannot ensure sustainable management of natural resources.

(b) **Three sector policy goals** are considered essential for sustainable agriculture and rural development:

- food security by ensuring an appropriate mix of self-sufficiency and self-reliance;
- employment and income generation in rural areas;
- natural resource conservation and environmental protection.

(c) **Three objectives** should guide the choice of options for sustainable agriculture and rural development:

- improving efficiency
- increasing resilience and minimizing risks
- promoting diversity

(d) **Four major options** are considered:

- intensification through specialization
- intensification through diversification
- combining on-farm and off-farm activities (pluriactivity)
- extensive systems

232. These options are not readily applicable in many cases, and the following major adjustments and changes may be required:

- decentralization by devolving more responsibility down to local level, by providing incentives for initiatives by local communities rather than relying on "top-down" administrative mechanisms;
- allocating clear rights with regard to resource use;
- relieving pressure on natural resources by undertaking improvement, rehabilitation and conservation work so that the resources can be used more intensively; encouraging demand for products which can be produced sustainably; and improving the man/land (and water) relationship through land reform and, where desirable and feasible, encouraging transmigration;
- using technologies adapted to sustainability objectives in order to provide relief at points where the environment is under particular pressure; providing farming system packages rather than handling each problem separately; seeking solutions in information technologies, good practices and know-how rather than in ever-increasing use of external inputs and hardware.

### 6.4.2 Coastal aquaculture and fisheries development

233. It is most important that coastal aquaculture planning and management give special emphasis to development efforts compatible with existing and projected conditions of inland aquaculture and capture fisheries, both coastal and inland (Bailey and Skladany, 1991). Effects of coastal aquaculture development on coastal fisheries resources and on consumer acceptance and marketability, especially distribution and marketing of fishery products, must be considered and forecasted. In some cases, it may even be required to limit expansion of coastal aquaculture in order to avoid detriment to coastal fisheries resource users, such as traditional small-scale fishery communities. Selection of aquaculture sites, methods and species should take account of both employment opportunities (part-time or full-time) for fishermen and local demands for species which are not provided by capture fisheries or which are caught only in insufficient amounts.

### 6.4.3 Coastal aquaculture and rural development

234. Coastal aquaculture development planners should, where required, actively participate in the formulation and implementation of trans-sectoral management plans aiming at coordinated land-use and resource development in coastal areas. The allocation of resources and potential sites to aquaculture and the selection of forms of aquaculture practice should be preceded by adequate on-site surveys and evaluations. It is important that coastal aquaculture development planners and experienced aquafarmers participate in coastal surveys leading to designation of zones with the resource uses specified.

235. Economic viability and social acceptability of existing aquaculture practices may be further promoted through increased horizontal and vertical integration within local economies. Aquafarmers may stimulate acceptance and support by stakeholders of other local activities when achieving agreements, for example, on changes in patterns of land and water use and waste disposal,

diversification of methods, use of agricultural by-products, promotion of the local marketing system, encouragement of locally-based processing facilities, etc.

### 6.4.4 Coastal aquaculture and environmental policies

236. Coastal aquaculture planning and management will, in many cases, have to take account of established national policies aiming at environmental protection. In aquaculture development plans, it should be stated how the general management framework adopted for the protection of coastal environments has been adapted to meet the specific needs and characteristics of aquaculture practices. Environmental protection requirements for aquaculture should also be integrated in development plans of other sectors. Requirements and specifications on environmental assessment and monitoring of aquaculture practices should form an integral part of an organized development plan which should also contain options for mitigation of environmental impacts. Environmentally-acceptable aquaculture practices may be prioritized in development plans. Coastal aquaculture development planners should actively participate in the formulation of environmental legislation governing aquaculture.

### 6.4.5 Support to coastal aquaculture and limitations of development

237. Government development strategies in support of sustainable aquaculture should give increased emphasis to environmental considerations when promoting the following aspects (Chua and Tech, 1990):

- demonstration of technical and economical feasibility of aquaculture systems with guidelines in the choice of appropriate species and culture systems and appropriate farm operating procedure;
- basic infrastructure in the aquaculture zone in terms of water supply and delivery, electricity, roads, post-harvest and marketing facilities;
- availability of credit facilities and insurance schemes for aquaculture investment;
- technical and management training for small farmers, technicians and managers;
- technology development and transfer, supported by appropriate research.

238. When formulating or modifying coastal aquaculture development plans, it may prove useful to specifically address limitations to development imposed by (i) the present state of aquaculture technology and expertise, (ii) prevailing socio-economic conditions, (iii) institutional and regulatory weaknesses, (iv) access to and availability of resources required, and (v) the current state of the coastal environment and its capacity to further assimilate effects of contamination and physical modifications.

## 6.5 Environmental Management Options at Farm or Project Level

239. It is emphasized that environmental management at farm level can be achieved essentially through proper planning and design, and in particular, through adequate site selection allowing for sufficient water exchange, and through rationalization in farm operation and maintenance, including adequate selection of species, suitable stocking rates, appropriate feeding regimes and careful use of aquachemicals. Constant monitoring of conditions of cultured stock, water quality, and hygienic circumstances, is required.

### 6.5.1 Aquaculture project formulation

240. Accurate planning is essential when formulating sustainable coastal aquaculture projects. Guidance material on aquaculture project formulation is available (Insull and Nash 1990; see also Eid 1986; FAO, 1989c). The Aquaculture Development and Coordination Programme (ADCP) published general guidelines for bioprogramming and design of an aquaculture facility (Brown and Nash, 1988). An elementary checklist for coastal aquaculture projects in tropical environments is

given in **Annex 11**. In designing and building a new aquaculture facility, especially when applying new technology untried in a particular area, it may be prudent to develop the new system in stages so as to permit any necessary changes to be easily and economically incorporated.

241. The following are ten project-oriented "principles" of sustainable development, which may help prevent environmental and developmental problems in coastal aquaculture (Brindley, 1991):

(1) **Consult with villagers, farmers and all other participants.** Reach agreement on both problems and solutions before taking action.

(2) **Plan small-scale, flexible projects.** A plan should be a blueprint, not a prison. It should be able to incorporate new information that emerges during the project.

(3) **Let the people benefitting from the project make the decisions.** The expert's job is to share their knowledge, not to impose it.

(4) **Look for solutions that can be duplicated in the hundreds of thousands** for the greatest impact on development. But the solutions must still be tailored to fit local needs.

(5) **Provide education and training,** particularly for young people and women, who remain the most effective agents of change because they are bound to the realities of the family's survival.

(6) **Keep external inputs to a minimum** to reduce dependency and increase stability. Subsidies, supplements and inappropriate technology are unsustainable.

(7) **Build on what people are doing right.** New ideas will be adopted only if they do not run contrary to local practice. New technologies must support existing ones, not replace them.

(8) **Assess impacts of proposed changes.** A multi-disciplinary team, ideally including specialists from the same culture, should look at economic, social, cultural and environmental aspects.

(9) **Consider both inputs and outcomes.** The failure of projects focusing on a single outcome, such as agricultural productivity, has proved that more is not always better.

(10) **Maintain or improve the participants' standard of living.** Long-term environmental improvements are unsustainable unless they also address the problems which the poor face today.

### 6.5.2 Adaptive and mitigatory measures

242. Properly sited and managed aquaculture activities should not result in unacceptable ecological change. Nevertheless, should change occur, measures can be taken to avoid or minimize it.

Rational use of mangrove wetland

243. GESAMP (1991c) recommends that the use of mangroves along the shore front or fringing river banks for aquaculture be discouraged in view of their significant contribution to coastal stability preventing soil erosion, and their role as valuable habitats. Unlike extensive shrimp farming in mangrove swamps utilizing tidal energy for water exchange and shrimp larvae supply, modern intensive shrimp farming uses mechanical pumps for water supply and seeds from hatcheries. As such the use of mangrove swamps for intensive shrimp culture cannot be justified in environmental terms. Traditional use of mangrove wetland for extensive aquaculture has minimal negative ecological impacts.

244. Burbridge *et al.* (1988) suggest the following approach for fish and shrimp pond construction in mangrove areas:

(1) In mangrove areas, the location of ponds inland from the mangrove should be considered as the first alternative.

(2) Rehabilitation of abandoned ponds and/or the improved management of existing ponds should also be considered before the clearance of additional mangrove areas is envisaged.

(3) Where there is no alternative to the conversion of mangrove, the following guidelines should be observed:

(a) avoid soils with high acid-sulphate potential;
(b) if this is unavoidable, incorporate into the pond design the ability to exchange approximately 25 percent of the pond water volume daily by either tidal exchange or pumping;
(c) if adequate exchange cannot be achieved, lime should be used to neutralize acids, or non-acid soils brought to the site to form the bunds and to line the ponds;
(d) do not site the ponds over tidal creeks because they are believed to form the primary habitat for the post-larval stage of several fish species normally cultivated in ponds; the creek beds also form poor foundations for bunds and slumping is likely to result;
(e) do not block tidal creeks and other channels which allow tidal flushing of adjacent mangrove;
(f) avoid the diversion of freshwater runoff away from the mangrove; where freshwater has to be diverted, it should be redirected to the mangrove by means of shallow channels along seaward margins of the ponds.

245. Kapetsky (1987a) emphasizes the need for long-term integrated management of mangrove areas. Frequently proposed remedies such as the intensification of pond culture in place of extensification, and the promotion of non-destructive aquaculture techniques such as pen, cage and raft culture as alternatives to pond culture, are often not acceptable because of technological end economic constraints. Thorhaug (1987; 1990; see also Coats and Williams, 1990) has reviewed methods and results of mangrove and seagrass restoration as a means to benefit fisheries and aquaculture, both ecologically and economically.

Waste management

246. Treatment of effluents may be required, particularly in intensive aquaculture systems. However, high volumetric flow rates and relatively dilute concentrations of contaminants in such effluents pose significant problems. Treatment technologies are being developed in industrialized countries based on sedimentation, decantation, biological oxidation and filtration (Warrer-Hansen, 1982; see also Petit and Maurel, 1983). Often, these techniques are designed for "high-tech" systems (see for example Mäkinen *et al.,* 1988; Cripps, in press; Beveridge *et al.,* 1991; Dryden, 1991). Huguenin and Colt (1989) review water-recycling approaches, including nitrification and biofilters, foam fractionation, carbon adsorption, ion exchange, algal systems and ozone.

247. Economic constraints in production and operating costs often make the treatment of farm wastes difficult to support (Muir, 1982), particularly in developing countries. Treatment facilities must be efficient, yet economically feasible to install and to operate. However, use of suitably designed sedimentation ponds appears to be a cost-efficient practice in many commercial farms. Whilst sedimentation methods are generally effective for the removal of suspended solids (Henderson and Bromage, 1988), the process itself may increase the rate of release of dissolved substances during solids decomposition (NCC, 1989). The sludge accumulated in sedimentation ponds or in culture ponds should be deposited on land on mud bunds of the ponds.

248. Removal of suspended matter from ponds may also be achieved in sedimentation ponds stocked with filter-feeding organisms, such as oysters or mussels. Nutrient loads can be reduced when seaweeds such as *Gracilaria* and *Caulerpa* are polycultured with shrimp or milkfish in ponds or cultivated in exit canals (Chua, in press). Integrated practices, for example, off-bottom polyculture of bivalves and seaweeds (Ruying and Qingyin, 1992), salmonid cage culture combined with mussel culture (Folke and Kautsky, 1989), use of mullets in bottom cages underneath seabream cages (Porter *et al.*, in press), or shrimp/oyster co-production systems (Wang, 1990) may prove very successful in reducing effects of waste loads from sea-based farms (see also Shpigel and Fridman, 1990).

249. Changing culture sites is an approach which may be used with sea-based aquafarms to avoid excessive accumulation of organic sediments. Site rotation may contribute to sediment recovery through natural dispersal and disintegration of wastes during periods where farming areas are left to lie fallow. Additional trawling of sediments is sometimes applied to assist oxygenation and mineralization of wastes. Sediment loadings per unit area may be reduced through single point mooring systems in cage farms (Ives, 1989).

250. Sophisticated technology, such as submersible pumps and mixers, and funnel-shaped waste catchment devices or collectors, is being experimented which perhaps may be used regularly in the future to collect or disperse organic wastes deposited (NCC, 1989; Weston, 1991).

251. Implementation of approaches such as site rotation and dispersal of sedimented waste may, however, appear undesirable in certain cases, since these practices may only result in the disturbance of a greater area of the bottom (Gowen *et al.,* 1990; Weston, 1991).

<u>Rational use of feeds and fertilizers</u>

252. Since inputs of fertilizers and, in particular, feeds are often the main cause of deterioration of environmental quality within and outside the culture unit, improvements are required in the management (i.e., choice, storage, handling and application) of these inputs. The reader is referred to existing relevant documentation such as, for example, Tacon (1988); New (1987); Tacon (1987a, 1987b). It is emphasized that the choice and adoption of appropriate "low-pollution" feeding methods and feeds will, in many cases, be governed by financial circumstances aquafarmers are facing.

253. Excessive use of inorganic and organic fertilizers should be avoided. Under farm conditions, it is difficult to precisely predict or adjust the degree of fertilization required. Monitoring of pond water quality should be carried out regularly. It is suggested to record time, frequency and mode of application as well as the type and amount of fertilizers applied. It should be ensured that fertilizers be well dispersed or diluted. Piedrahita and Giovannini (1991) discuss new developments in the engineering and management of fertilized non-fed pond systems.

254. Unfortunately, to date there is little or no information on the dietary nutrient requirements of warmwater fish or shrimp species under semi-intensive pond farming conditions, or concerning the natural food productivity of ponds with different management (i.e., water, aeration, fertilizer and feed) techniques (Tacon, in press). However, direct transfer and application of intensive complete diet feeding strategies to semi-intensive pond farming systems is current practice. For example, at present almost all commercial shrimp farmers in Latin America and Asia employ a complete diet feeding strategy for their semi-intensive shrimp ponds with no provision within the artificial diets used for natural food availability (Tacon, in press). Clearly, this situation must be remedied if farmers are to reduce both production costs and feed-derived waste loadings to the environment.

255. It cannot be over-emphasized that feeding regimes need to be adapted to specific feeding habits and behaviour of cultured species, particularly in intensive (feed-lot) farming systems. Ideally, feed inputs should be determined based on knowledge of species-specific feeding behaviour and

nutritional requirements as well as on estimates of biomass in the culture units. However, calculation of optimum feeding rates is problematic since appropriate methods to accurately assess exact weight and number of stock per culture unit still need to be developed.

256. In many cases, feed wastage due to over-feeding can be reduced by careful hand-feeding. Feed supply by automatic feeders should be closely monitored. It may be required that feeds be evenly dispersed over the culture unit, or feeding strategy may have to be adjusted according to territorial behaviour of cultured stock or water currents prevailing in the culture unit.

257. Meticulous recording is suggested of amount and type (e.g., trash fish, compound feeds, water content, chemical composition, particle size, etc.) of feeds given, of feeding methods and devices (hand-feeding, demand/automatic feeders, boat feeding, feed blowers, etc.) as well as of feeding time and frequency per day or of any change in feeding strategy, such as position of operator/feeder as related to the culture unit. Feeding response of cultured stock should, where possible, also be observed. With this information recorded, the significance of farm-specific food conversion ratio (FCR) values may be increased as the parameter relevant for assessment of feeding efficiency.

258. Feed losses in salmonid cage culture have been reduced by the use of slow sinking feed pellets and, more recently in Scandinavia, by the introduction of floating pellets which are released from the base of the cages and float slowly to the surface (NCC, 1989). These floating pellets allow feed wastage to be monitored and uneaten pellets to be removed. Such techniques, which aim at maximizing the opportunity for ingestion of pellets, are still very much at the development stage, but may have potential for significantly reducing solid loadings. However, dispersal by currents of uncaptured pellets over wider areas may be considered advantageous or disadvantageous for the environment. As related to the water content of pellets, NCC (1989) recommends that the use of moist or wet diets be discouraged in Scottish salmonid culture.

259. Currently, increasing attention is also being directed to reducing waste output through development of nutritional strategies aiming at improved composition of feeds for intensive aquaculture as carried out in temperate countries. These strategies include the application of biotechnology to pre-processing of feed ingredients to increase digestibility and aim at attaining optimal nutrient and energy balance in the diet thereby leading to high nutrient retention. Cho *et al.* (1991) state that diets which are highly digestible, of high nutrient density and with a well-balanced protein:energy ratio are the most desirable feed. However, it is also stated, that feed cost per unit of fish production must, at the same time, be acceptable to the market place. An overview on current discussions and experiences related to improved feed formulation and processing for intensive aquaculture in temperate countries can be found in Cowey and Cho (1991). The reader is further referred to Akiyama (1991); Jensen (1991); Enell and Ackefors (1991); Carter (1991); Seymour and Bergheim (1991); Clarke (1990); New (1990b, 1989).

<u>Chemical usage</u>

260. Aquaculture chemicals including biocides and biostats, chemicals in construction materials, etc., should be used with extreme care. With environmental awareness growing worldwide, it can be expected that the issue of chemical usage in aquaculture will become a very significant criterion influencing consumer acceptance and marketability of aquaculture products.

261. Farmers should be encouraged to reduce, as far as possible, all treatments required through the use of sound husbandry practices aiming at stress prevention, including careful minimal handling and, in particular, avoidance of over-stocking (NCC, 1989). More emphasis should be given to preventive measures, especially in intensive culture systems. Use of chemicals should be considered as the last tool when other measures have proven inadequate.

262. Prevention of diseases should, wherever possible, include strict quality control of stocking material; proper storage, handling and application of feeds; regular water-quality monitoring and

inspection of species; early detection of unusual behaviuor, loss of appetite, etc. and segregation or removal of any sick or dead farmed organism. Biological control methods, such as the use of wrasse species (*Ctenolabrus spp.*) to remove lice parasites on Norwegian salmon, may help to reduce application of hazardous chemicals (Anonymus, 1990).

263. Prophylactic use of antibiotics should be avoided and antibiotics should be administered only for the purpose of curing infectious disease (ADB/NACA, 1991; Braaten and Hektoen, 1991). The environmental risks involved may be reduced by limiting exposure to specific drugs, through, for example, modified formulations, avoidance of frequent use of a single compound, rotation of drugs, changes in application methods, and due timing of applications.

264. For proper aquaculture drug use in Canada, it has been recommended (Johnson and Ronnie, 1989, quoted in Schnick, 1991) that the aquafarmer (1) obtain an accurate diagnosis, (2) use an appropriate compound and route of administration, (3) use doses for the minimum time, (4) keep records and evaluate treatments, and (5) be aware of residues. Evidently, specialized expertise is required to assist aquafarmers in the diagnosis of disease problems, in improved disease-preventing farm operation and appropriate use of drugs.

265. It may be desirable to establish public aquaculture health management services which may cover requirements for quarantine, diagnosis, treatment, monitoring and product quality control. It should be ensured that related efforts also benefit small-scale aquafarmers, for example, through training and extension.

266. Farmers should keep records on chemical usage, including type, amount and combinations of chemicals used; reasons for application; mode, frequency, start and end of administrations; amount/number and sizes of stock treated; and time of harvesting of treated stock. Safe storage and disposal of chemicals are essential.

267. Ideally, detailed inventories of chemicals used should be established for use by designated authorities. Registration, marketing licences and other control requirements may be imposed on those importing, manufacturing, processing (e.g., feed producers) or selling hazardous compounds. Aquafarmers buying produce containing potentially hazardous compounds should be provided with understandable information for appropriate use including warning statements, contra-indications for use, dosage recommendations, treatment procedures, drug retention times, recommended withdrawal times, etc. The reader is further referred to FAO/WHO, 1991a; ICES, 1990; Bernoth, 1991b; Ellis, 1991; Meyer and Schnick, 1989; Schnick *et al.*, 1989; Williams and Lightner, 1988).

### Decontamination

268. It is due to the capacity of bivalves to concentrate and accumulate pathogenic micro-organisms and chemical substances from polluted waters, coupled with the tradition of consuming shellfish raw or only lightly cooked, that bivalve molluscs present a risk for the unwary consumer.

269. Several measures are being implemented or tested to prevent related human health problems (Canzonier, 1988; Thrower, 1990). Documentation on experiences with depuration and sanitation of shellfish in developing and industrialized countries can be found in NACA (1989) and Otwell *et al.* (1991).

270. Methods of post-harvest heat treatment of bivalves, ranging from steam blanching to full sterilization in processes such as canning, are appropriate only for bivalves which contain heat labile contaminants and which are acceptable by the consumer as cooked products. Application of several marinading solutions may help to wash off bacteria and clay particles holding heavy metals from the gills and feeding palps. Irradiation techniques, though costly, may be used to sterilize products, but may result in undesirable changes in flavour, odour and texture.

271. Relaying is the harvesting of the shellfish from a contaminated site and allowing them to

purge themselves of contaminants in unpolluted waters for relatively long periods. This practice, which may indeed achieve effective removal of some contaminants such as heavy metals, is, however, time- and labor-intensive.

272. In depuration processes, the animals are transferred to special tanks with constant or frequent exchange of clean seawater whereupon pathogens are supposedly eliminated. The efficacy/duration of the process is quite variable, depending on the nature of the contaminant, the species being depurated, the metabolic rate of the species, and the water quality in the tank.

273. Without adequate disinfection systems, depuration may serve to spread pathogens from a few contaminated animals to many others in the depuration system. Seawater is therefore often sterilized by using chlorine, ozone or ultraviolet light. However, high levels of chlorine may well inactivate many pathogens but may also adversely affect the animals. With some disinfectants, the animals close up, and, therefore, do not depurate. Although costly, ozonation appears to be an effective method. Moreover, residual ozone in the water, which does not adversely affect the filter-feeders, results in the inactivation of bacterial fish pathogens, certain parasites and, possibly, viruses, including *poliovirus* (GESAMP, 1991c). Controversy still rages over whether or not depuration will remove pathogenic viruses (Thrower, 1990). Use of ultraviolet light is most widely used, and has the advantage of relative low costs and the absence of residual taints and odours from chemical residuals (Thrower, 1990).

274. However, depuration on a small-scale is not economically feasible, and may require a collaborative operation by aquafarmers and processing industry, possibly supported by public authorities. The use of the process also imposes severe time restraints in marketing procedures and may require the application of stringent control measures in the handling and distribution of the depurated product. Canzonier (1988) emphasizes that operational requirements for effective depuration are so onerous that they are frequently either circumvented or the process is abandoned altogether.

275. Other types of contaminants such as certain hydrocarbons, heavy metals and biotoxins, may be so avidly sequestered in the tissues of the bivalve that the depuration process is virtually useless in reducing them to acceptable levels. Shumway (1990, 1989) reviewed attempts to detoxify shellfish contaminated with phycotoxins aiming at reducing the duration of "off-market" times. While relaying is satisfactory for many species, toxin retention times vary considerably between species, and some species remain toxic for extended periods. Ozonation may prove effective in some cases, while it is useless in detoxifying bivalves that have ingested algal cysts or have had the toxins bound in their tissues over longer periods. At present, the economic feasibility of efficiently detoxifying shellfish on a large scale basis in artificial systems is not promising (Shumway, 1990).

276. In Japan and other countries, application of chemicals such as peroxocarbonate, cupric sulphate, formalin and others, is being considered to remove red tide organisms (Okaichi, 1991). Even though the use of such chemicals may be restricted to aquaculture ponds or very limited water areas, ecological and economic feasibility of this type of countermeasure remains to be thoroughly assessed. In view of the increasing number of algal bloom events, Maclean (1991) emphasizes the need for monitoring of shellfish and/or plankton combined with hydrographic research as well as public education.

277. Algal bloom countermeasures at farm level may include (Black, 1988): (i) provision of multiple water intakes (e.g., pumping of plankton-free water from various depths); (ii) vertical movement of cultured organisms (e.g., sinking of cages); (iii) relocating of culture units to unaffected areas which requires detachable moorings and towable structures; (iv) pre-emptive harvesting; (v) reduction of food supply and stress to lower metabolism of cultured stock; (vi) on-site shielding of stock (e.g., bubble curtains, injection of clear water, non-porous barriers); (vii) cortisone treatment to reduce gill-swelling.

278. In concluding, it appears that efforts directed at decontamination of aquaculture produce may, in many cases, be the second best option to cope with problems related to coastal water pollution and algal bloom events. Aquaculture production in unpolluted waters and low risk areas combined with effective hazard assessment and regular monitoring should be promoted. Public awareness programmes may urge consumers to eat only cooked seafood without entrails and gills, specifying periods and species for safe consumption. Unfortunately, in some cases, it may be necessary to enforce temporary bans on harvesting, transporting and marketing of possibly contaminated shellfish.

## 7. REFERENCES

Ackefors, H. and M. Enell, 1990. Discharge of nutrients from Swedish fish farming to adjacent sea areas. Ambio, 19(1):28-35

Ackefors, H., V. Hilge, and O. Linden, 1990. Contaminants in shellfish and fish products. Eur.Aquacult.Soc.Spec.Publ., (12):305-44

ADB, 1988. Guidelines for integrated regional economic-cum-environmental development planning. A review of regional environmental development planning studies in Asia. Vol 2: Case studies. Manila, Asian Dev.Bank Environ.Pap., (3.2).

ADB, 1991a. Environmental guidelines for selected agricultural and natural resources development projects. Manila, Asian Development Bank, 115 p.

ADB, 1991b. Guidelines for integrated regional economic-cum-environmental development planning. A review of regional environmental development planning studies in Asia. Vol 1: Guidelines. Manila, Asian Dev.Bank Environ.Pap., (3.1):125 p.

ADB/NACA, 1991. Environmental aspects of fish health management. In Fish health management in Asia-Pacific. Report on a regional study and workshop on fish disease and fish health management. Bangkok, Network of Aquaculture Centres in Asia-Pacific. Asian Dev.Bank Agricult.Dep.Rep.Ser., (1):34-7

ADCP, 1989. Planning for aquaculture development. Report of an expert consultation held in Policoro, Italy. 26 July - 2 August 1988. UNDP/FAO Aquaculture Development and Coordination Programme. Rome, FAO. ADCP/REP/89/33:68 p.

Ahmad, Y.J. and G.K. Sammy, 1985. Guidelines to environmental impact assessment in developing countries. Sponsored by United Nations Environment Programme. London, Hodder and Stoughton, 52 p.

Aitken, D., 1990. Shrimp farming in Ecuador. An aquaculture success story. World Aquacult., 21(1):7-16

Akiyama, D.M., 1991. Future considerations for the aquaculture feed industry. In Proceedings of the aquaculture feed processing and nutrition workshop, held 19-25 September 1991 in Thailand and Indonesia; edited by D.M. Akiyama and R.K.H. Tan. Singapore, American Soybean Association, pp 5-9

Akiyama, D.M. and N.L.M. Chwang, 1989. Shrimp feed requirements and feed management. In Proceedings of the Southeast Asia shrimp farm management workshop, held in the Philippines, Indonesia, Thailand. 26 July - 11 August 1989; edited by D.M. Akiyama. Singapore, American Soybean Association, pp 75-82

Andriawan, E. and H. Jhamtani, 1989. Mangrove forest destruction in Indonesia and its impact on community system. In Symposium on mangrove management: Its ecological and economic considerations, held in Bogor, Indonesia, 9-11 August, 1988. Bogor, Southeast Asian Regional Center for Tropical Biology (SEAMEO - BIOTROP). BIOTROP Spec.Publ., (37):245-52

Angell, C., 1991. Oyster culture in tropical Asia. INFOFISH Int., 4/91:47-51

Apud, F., J.H. Primavera and P.L. Torres, 1983. Farming of prawns and shrimps. Tigbauan, Iloilo, Southeast Asian Fisheries Development Center, Aquaculture Extension Manual No.5.

Archer, J.A., 1988. Coastal Management in the United States: A selective review and summary. Rhode Island, USAID and Coastal Resources Center at the University of Rhode Island. International Coastal Resources Management Project; 24 p.

Arthur, R. and M. Shariff, 1991. Towards international fish disease control in Southeast Asia. INFOFISH Int., 3/91:45-8

Aure, J. and A. Stigebrandt, 1990. Quantitative estimates of the eutrophication effects of fish farming on fjords. Aquaculture, 90:135-56

Bailey, C., 1988. The social consequences of tropical shrimp mariculture development. Ocean Shoreline Manage., 11:31-44

Bailey, C. and M. Skladany, 1991. Aquacultural development in tropical Asia: A re-evaluation. Nat.Resour. Forum, 15(1):66-73

Bailly, D., 1989. Economic and social aspects of shellfish basin management. In Aquaculture: A review of recent experience. Paris, Organization for Economic Cooperation and Development (OECD), pp 314-27

Baltz, D.M., 1991. Introduced fishes in marine systems and inland seas. Biol.Conserv., 56:151-77

Baluyut, E.A., 1989. Aquaculture systems and practices: a selected review. Rome, UNDP/FAO Aquaculture Development and Coordination Programme. ADCP/REP/89/43:90 p.

Baluyut, E.A., 1991. Fish disease and fish health management: environmental aspects. In Fish health management in Asia-Pacific. Report on a regional study and workshop on fish disease and fish health management. Bangkok, Network of Aquaculture Centres in Asia-Pacific. Asian Dev.Bank Agricult.Dep.Rep.Ser., (1):607-14

Bashirullah, A.K.M., N. Mahmood and A.K.M.A. Matin, 1989. Aquaculture and coastal zone management in Bangladesh. Coast.Manage., 17:119-27

Baticados, M.C.L. *et al.*, 1990. Diseases of penaeid shrimps in the Philippines. Tigbauan, Iloilo, Southeast Asian Fisheries Development Center, Aquaculture Extension Manual No. 16.

Bendavid-Val, A., 1990. Rural area development planning; A review and synthesis of approaches. FAO training materials for agricultural planning. Rome, FAO. ESP/TMAP/21:287 p.

Bergheim, A. and O.I. Forsberg, 1992. Attempts to reduce effluent loadings from salmon farms by varying feeding frequencies and mechanical effluent treatment. Paper presented at BORDEAUX AQUACULTURE '92; Bordeaux, France, 25-27 March 1992.

Bergstrom, J.C., 1991. Concepts and measures of the economic value of environmental quality: a review. J.Environ.Manage., 31:215-28

Bernoth, E.M. (Editor), 1991a. Public health aspects of seafood-borne zoonotic diseases. Proceedings of the WHO Symposium held in Hannover, Germany, 14-16 November 1989. Berlin, Institut fur Veterinarmedizin. Vet.Med. Hefte (1/1991):144 p.

Bernoth, E.M., 1991b. Possible hazards due to fish drugs. In Public health aspects of seafood-borne zoonotic diseases. Proceedings of the WHO Symposium held in Hannover, Germany, 14-16 November 1989, edited by E.M. Bernoth. Berlin, Institut fur Veterinarmedizin. Vet.Med. Hefte (1/1991):129-35

Beveridge, M.C.M., 1984. Cage and pen fish farming. Carrying capacity models and environmental impact. FAO Fish.Tech.Pap., (255):131 p.

Beveridge, M.C.M., 1987. Cage culture. Surrey, Fishing News Books Ltd., 351 p.

Beveridge, M.C.M., M.J. Phillips and R.M. Clarke, 1991. A quantitative and qualitative assessment of wastes from aquatic animal production. In Aquaculture and water quality, edited by D.E. Brune and J.R. Tomasso. Baton Rouge, World Aquaculture Society. Adv.World Aquacult., (3):506-33

Biney, C. *et al.*, 1987. Scientific bases for pollution control in African inland waters. Chem.Ecol., (3):49-74

Bird, K., 1989. Intensive seaweed cultivation. Aquacult.Mag., 15(6):29-34

Bisset, R., 1983. Methods for environmental impact assessment: A selective survey with case studies. In Environmental Impact Assessment for Developing Countries, edited by A.K. Biswas and Q. Geping. International Society for Ecological Modelling, United Nations University in Guangzhou, People's Republic of China and United Nations Environment Programme, pp 5-64

Bisset, R., 1989. Introduction to EIA methods. Paper presented at 10th International Seminar on Environmental Impact Assessment and Management; 9-22 July 1989, University of Aberdeen, Scotland.

Bjorklund, H., J. Bondestam and G. Bylund, 1990. Residues of oxytetracycline in wild fish and sediments from fish farms. Aquaculture, 86:359-67

Black, E., 1988. Integrated management of plankton problems. In Proceedings of the workshop on exceptional marine blooms: their impact on fisheries and aquaculture, edited by W.E. Lorne Clayton. Bamfield Marine Station, 5-7 June 1988. Victoria, B.C., Ministry of Agriculture and Fisheries, pp 1-6

Black, E.A., (in press). Coastal resources inventories: A Pacific coast strategy for aquaculture development. Eur.Aquacult.Soc.Spec.Publ., (16)

Boudou, A. and F. Ribeyre, 1989. Fundamental concepts in aquatic ecotoxicology. In Aquatic ecotoxicology: fundamental concepts and methodologies, edited by A. Boudou and F. Ribeyre. Boca Raton, Florida, CRC Press. Vol. 1:35-76

Bower, S.B. and A.J. Figueras, 1989. Infectious diseases of mussels, especially pertaining to mussel transplantation. World Aquacult., 20(4):89-93

Braaten, B. and H. Hektoen, 1991. The environmental impact of aquaculture. In Fish health management in Asia-Pacific. Report on a regional study and workshop on fish disease and fish health management. Bangkok, Network of Aquaculture Centres in Asia-Pacific. Asian Dev.Bank Agricult.Dep.Rep.Ser., (1):469-524

Brindley, B., 1991. What is "sustainable" ? Some rules for the development road. Ceres, (128):35-8

Bro-Rasmussen, F. and K. Christiansen, 1984. Hazard Assessment - A summary of analysis and integrated evaluation of exposure and potential effects from toxic environmental chemicals. Ecol.Modell., 22:67-84

Brock, J.A., 1991. An overview of diseases of cultured crustaceans in the Asia Pacific Region. In Fish health management in Asia-Pacific. Report on a regional study and workshop on fish disease and fish health management. Bangkok, Network of Aquaculture Centres in Asia-Pacific. Asian Dev.Bank Agricult.Dep.Rep.Ser., (1):347-95

Brown, C.M. and C.E. Nash, 1988. Planning an aquaculture facility - Guidelines for bioprogramming and design. Rome, UNDP/FAO Aquaculture Development and Coordination Programme. ADCP/REP/87/24:41 p.

Brown, J.H., 1989. Antibiotics: their use and abuse in aquaculture. World Aquacult., 20(2):34-43

Brown, J.R., R.J. Gowen and D.S. McLusky, 1987. The effect of salmon farming on the benthos of a Scottish sea loch. J.Exp.Mar.Biol., 109:39-51

Burbridge, P., 1991. Integrated coastal zone management. In The status of integrated coastal zone management: a global assessment. Report on a special workshop held in July 1989 in Charleston, S.C., USA; edited by J.R. Clark. The Coastal Area Management and Planning Network (CAMPNET). Rosenstiel School of Marine and Atmospheric Sciences at the University of Miami, USA; pp 105-9

Burbridge, P.R., R.B. Norgaard and G.S. Hartshorn, 1988. Environmental guidelines for resettlement projects in the humid tropics. FAO Environ.Energy Pap., (9):67 p.

Butler, M.J.A. *et al.*, 1988. The application of remote sensing technology to marine fisheries: an introductory manual. FAO Fish.Tech.Pap., (295):165 p.

Bye, V.J., 1990. Legal, political and social constraints in aquaculture. Eur.Aquacult.Soc.Spec.Publ., (12):123-44

Cai, Y. and X. Li, 1990. Oyster culture in the People's Republic of China. World Aquacult., 21(4):67-72

Cairns, J., 1977. Aquatic ecosystem assimilative capacity. Fisheries, 2(2):5-7

Cairns, J., 1989. Applied ecotoxicology and methodology. In Aquatic ecotoxicology: fundamental concepts and methodologies, edited by A. Boudou and F. Ribeyre. Boca Raton, Florida, CRC Press. Vol. 2:275-90

Cairns, J., K.L. Dickson and A.W. Maki (Editors), 1978. Estimating the hazard of chemical substances to aquatic life. Summary and conclusions. ASTM Spec.Tech.Publ., (657):278 p.

Canzonier, W.J., 1988. Public health component of bivalve shellfish production and marketing. J.Shellfish Res., 7(2):261-6

Carpenter, R.A. and J.E. Maragos, 1989. How to assess environmental impacts on tropical islands and coastal areas. A training manual prepared for the South Pacific Regional Environment Programme (SPREP). Sponsored by the Asian Development Bank. Honolulu, East-West Center, 345 p.

Carter, C., 1991. Better nutrition means better ecology - or does it ? Fish Farmer, May/June 1991:24

Cendrero, A., 1989a. Mapping and evaluation of coastal areas for planning. Ocean Shoreline Manage., 12:427-62

Cendrero, A., 1989b. Land-use problems, planning and management in the coastal zone: An introduction. Ocean Shoreline Manage., 12:367-81

Chamberlain, G.W., 1991. Shrimp farming in Indonesia. I. - Growout techniques. World Aquacult., 22(2):12-27

Chantadisai, T., 1989. Environmental impact of aquaculture on mangrove ecosystem. In Symposium on mangrove management: Its ecological and economic considerations, held in Bogor, Indonesia, 9-11 August, 1988. Bogor, Southeast Asian Regional Center for Tropical Biology (SEAMEO - BIOTROP). BIOTROP Spec.Publ., (37):215-23

Charlier, R.H., 1989. Coastal zone: Occupance, management and economic competitiveness. Ocean Shoreline Manage., 12:383-402

Chen, D., 1989. Coastal zone development, utilization, legislation, and management in China. Coast.Manage., 17:55-62

Chen, J.X., 1991. Seaweed diseases in phycoculture systems. In Fish health management in Asia-Pacific. Report on a regional study and workshop on fish disease and fish health management. Bangkok, Network of Aquaculture Centres in Asia-Pacific. Asian Dev.Bank Agricult.Dep.Rep.Ser., (1):583-92

Chew, K.K., 1989. Recent trends in bivalve culture in the orient. Aquacult.Mag., 15(3):41-54

Chew, K.K., 1990. Global bivalve shellfish introductions. World Aquacult., 21(3):9-22

Chia, L.S., K. Habibullah and L.M. Chou (Editors), 1988. The coastal environmental profile of Singapore. Manila, ASEAN/US Coastal Resources Management Project; Technical Publications Series No.3. ICLARM Tech.Rep., (21):92 p.

Chien, Y.H., I.C. Liao and C.M. Yang, 1988. The evolution of prawn growout systems and their management in Taiwan. In Aquaculture engineering technologies for the future, edited by K. Murray. New York, Hemisphere Publishing Corporation. Inst.Chem.Eng.Symp.Ser., (111):143-68

Cho, C.Y. *et al.*, 1991. Quantitation of fish culture wastes by biological (nutritional) and chemical (iimnological) methods; the development of high nutrient dense (HND) diets. In Nutritional strategies and aquaculture waste. Proceedings of the First International Symposium on Nutritional Strategies in Management of Aquaculture Waste, edited by C.B. Cowey and C.Y. Cho. Guelph, Ontario, University of Guelph, pp 37-50

Cholik, F. and A. Poernomo, 1987. Development of aquaculture in mangrove areas and its relationship to the mangrove ecosystem. FAO Fish.Rep., (370)Suppl.:93-104

Chong, K.C., 1990a. Asian shrimp aquaculture - at cross roads. INFOFISH Int., 5/90:40-7

Chong, K.C., 1990b. Economic and social considerations for aquaculture site selection: An Asian perspective. In Technical and economic aspects of shrimp farming. Proceedings of the AQUATECH'90 Conference, Kuala Lumpur, Malaysia, 11-14 June 1990, edited by M.B. New, H. de Saram and T. Singh. Organized by Infofish in collaboration with the Fisheries Development Authority of Malaysia; pp 24-35

Chong, K.C. and I. Manwan, 1987. Incorporating integrated rural development into coastal resources use and management. In Pengelolaan dan Pola Perubahan Kawasan Pantai Utara Jawa. Studi Kasus Penelitian Agro-ecosistem. Kelompok Penelitian Agro-ecosistem (KEPAS). Badan Penelitian dan Penembangan Pertanian. Departemen Pertanian. [Management and its transformation in the North Coast of Java, Indonesia. Case studies on agro-ecosystem research. Working group on agro-ecosystem research (KEPAS). Agency for Agricultural Research and Development. Ministry of Agriculture]. Jakarta, Indonesia; pp 131-69

Chua, T.E., 1982. Marine cage culture systems in the tropics: Technology and potential. CIFA Tech.Pap., (9):228-59

Chua, T.E., 1989. Will coastal area management programs work in South East Asia ? ICLARM Conf.Proc., (19):231-40

Chua, T.E., 1991. Managing coastal resources for sustainable development: The ASEAN initiative. ICLARM Conf.Proc., (30):21-35

Chua, T.E., (in press). Environmental management of coastal aquaculture development. Contribution to the ICLARM Conference on Environment and Third World Aquaculture Development, held 17-22 September 1990 in Bellagio, Italy. Manila, International Center for Living Aquatic Resources Management.

Chua, T.E. and D. Pauly (Editors), 1989. Coastal area management in South East Asia: policies, management strategies and case studies. ICLARM Conf.Proc., (19): 254 p.

Chua, T.E. and L.F. Scura (Editors), 1991. Managing ASEAN's coastal resources for sustainable development: roles of policymakers, scientists, donors, media and communities. ICLARM Conf.Proc., (30):125 p.

Chua, T.E. and E. Tech, 1990. Aquaculture in Asia: Quo Vadis? In Aquaculture in Asia, edited by M.M. Joseph. Mangalore, Asian Fisheries Society, Indian Branch, pp 13-30

Chua, T.E., L.M. Chou and M.S.M. Sadorra (Editors), 1987. The coastal environmental profile of Brunei Darussalam: Resource assessment and management issues. Fisheries Department, Ministry of Development, Brunei Darussalam; ASEAN/US Coastal Resources Management Project. ICLARM Tech.Rep., (18):193 p.

Chua, T.E., J.N. Paw and F.Y. Guarin, 1989. The environmental impact of aquaculture and the effects of pollution on coastal aquaculture development in Southeast Asia. Mar.Pollut.Bull., 20(7):335-43

Clark, J.R. (Editor), 1991. The status of integrated coastal zone management: a global assessment. Report on a special workshop held in July 1989 in Charleston, S.C., USA. The Coastal Area Management and Planning Network (CAMPNET). Rosenstiel School of Marine and Atmospheric Sciences at the University of Miami, USA, 120 p.

Clarke, S., 1990. Extruded diets and pollution reduction. Fish Farmer, 4(1):95

Coats, R. and P. Williams, 1990. Hydrologic techniques for coastal wetland restoration illustrated by two case studies. In Environmental Restoration. Science and Strategies for Restoring the Earth, edited by J.J. Berger. Washington, D.C., Island Press, pp 236-46

Cowey, C.B. and C.Y. Cho (Editors), 1991. Nutritional strategies and aquaculture waste. Proceedings of the First International Symposium on Nutritional Strategies in Management of Aquaculture Waste. Guelph, Ontario, University of Guelph, 275 p.

Cripps, S.J., (in press). Comparison of methods for the removal of suspended particles from aquaculture effluents. Eur.Aquacult.Soc.Spec.Publ., (16)

Csavas, I., (in press). Aquaculture development and environmental issues in the developing countries of Asia. Contribution to the ICLARM Conference on Environment and Third World Aquaculture Development. Bellagio, Italy, 17-22 September 1990. Manila, International Center for Living Aquatic Resources Management.

Dahlback,B. and L.A.H. Gunnarsson, 1981. Sedimentation and sulphate reduction under a mussel culture. Mar.Biol., 63:269-75

Dixon, J.A., 1989. Valuation of mangroves. Trop.Coast.Area Manage., 4(3):1-6

Dixon, J.A. and M.M. Hufschmidt (Editors), 1986. Economic valuation techniques for the environment. A case study work book. Baltimore and London, The John Hopkins University Press, 203 p.

Dixon, J.A. *et al.*, 1986. Economic analysis of the environmental impacts of development projects. Manila, Asian Development Bank. Asian Dev.Bank Econ.Staff Pap., (31):100 p.

Dore, I., 1991. Shellfish: A guide to oysters, mussels, scallops, clams and similar products for the commercial user. New York, Van Nostrand Reinhold, 240 p.

Driver, P. and R. Bisset, 1989. The EIA process. In Report of workshops on environmental impact assessment, held in Pakistan, 16 September - 2 October 1989. Environment and Urban Affairs Division of the Government of Pakistan and IUCN-The World Conservation Union. Karachi, JRC-IUCN Pakistan, pp 5-11

Dryden, D., 1991. Water treatment enhances productivity as well as environment. Fish Farmer, 14(3):17-8

Egidius, E. and B. Moster, 1987. Effect of Neguvon and Nuvan treatment on crabs (*Cancer pagurus, C. maenas*), lobster (*Homarus gammarus*) and blue mussel (*Mytilus edulis*). Aquaculture, 60:165-8

Eid, M.A., 1986. The project cycle. FAO Investm.Cent.Tech.Pap., (4):16 p.

Ellis, A.E., 1991. Tissue residues of chemotherapeutants in cage-cultured fish. In Public health aspects of seafood-borne zoonotic diseases. Proceedings of the WHO Symposium held in Hannover, Germany, 14-16 November 1989, edited by E.M. Bernoth. Berlin, Institut fur Veterinarmedizin. Vet.Med. Hefte (1/1991):136-44

Enell, M. and H. Ackefors, 1991. Nutrient discharges from aquaculture operations in Nordic countries into adjacent sea areas. International Council for the Exploration of the Sea (ICES). C.M. 1991/F:56. Ref.MEQC., 17 p.

ERL, 1990. Environmental assessment procedures in the UN system. A study prepared at the request of the United Nations system, funded by UNEP. London, Environmental Resources Limited, 54 p.

ESCAP, 1985. Environmental impact assessment. Guidelines for planners and decision makers. Bangkok, United Nations Economic and Social Commission for Asia and the Pacific. ESCAP Environ.Dev.Ser. (ST/ESCAP/351):198 p.

FAO, 1985a. Mangrove management in Thailand, Malaysia and Indonesia. FAO Environ.Pap., (4):60 p.

FAO, 1985b. Applications of remote sensing to aquaculture and inland fisheries. Ninth UN/FAO International Training Course in Co-operation with the Government of Italy. Rome, Italy, 10-28 September 1984. FAO Remote Sens.Cent.Ser., (27):290 p.

FAO, 1988. Aspects of FAO's policies, programmes, budget and activities aimed at contributing to sustainable development. Document to the ninety-fourth Session of the FAO Council, Rome, 15-25 November 1988. Rome, FAO. CL 94/6.

FAO, 1989a. Contribution of remote sensing to marine fisheries. Twelfth UN/FAO International Training Course in Co-operation with the Government of Italy. Rome, Italy, 11-30 May 1987. FAO Remote Sens.Cent.Ser., (49):355 p.

FAO, 1989b. Guidelines for land use planning. FAO inter-departmental working group on land use planning. Rome, FAO, 121 p.

FAO, 1989c. The design of agricultural investment projects. Lessons from experience. FAO Investm.Cent.Tech.Pap., (6):59 p. plus annexes.

FAO, 1990. The definition of aquaculture and collection of statistics. FAO Aquacult.Min., (7):4 p.

FAO, 1991a. Aquaculture production (1986-1989). FAO Fish.Circ., (815)Rev.3:141 p.

FAO, 1991b. Land use planning applications. Proceedings of the FAO expert consultation held 10-14 December 1990 in Rome, Italy. FAO World Soil Resour.Rep., (68):206 p.

FAO, 1991c. Development of coastal areas and enclosed seas. Research Paper No.4, commissioned for the preparation of official reports for the United Nations Conference on Environment and Development. Geneva, UNCED Secretariat, 27 p.

FAO, 1992. Aquaculture production (1984-1990). FAO Fish.Circ., (815)Rev.4:206 p.

FAO/Netherlands, 1991a. Elements for strategies and agenda for action (draft proposal). Strategies and tools for sustainable agriculture and rural development. FAO/Netherlands Conference on Agriculture and the Environment, held 15-19 April 1991 in 'S-Hertogenbosch, The Netherlands. Rome, FAO, 27 p. plus appendices.

FAO/Netherlands, 1991b. Criteria, instruments and tools for sustainable agriculture and rural development. FAO/Netherlands Conference on Agriculture and the Environment, held 15-19 April 1991 in 'S-Hertogenbosch, The Netherlands. Rome, FAO. Main document No. 4. 36 p.

FAO/WHO, 1991a. Proposed draft code of hygienic practice for the products of aquaculture. FAO/WHO Codex Alimentarius Commission. Codex Committee on Fish and Fishery Products. Rome, FAO. CL 1991/28-FFP: 31 p.

FAO/WHO, 1991b. Proposed draft code of practice for the use of veterinary drugs in aquaculture. FAO/WHO Codex Alimentarius Commission. Joint FAO/WHO Food Standards Programme. Sixth Session of the Codex Committee on Residues of Veterinary Drugs in Foods, held 22-25 October 1991 in Washington, D.C., USA. Rome, FAO. CX/RVDF 91/9: 10 p.

Figueras, A.J., 1989. Mussel culture in Spain and France. World Aquacult., 20(4):8-17

Folke, C., 1988. Energy economy of salmon aquaculture in the Baltic sea. Environ.Manage., 12(4):525-37

Folke, C. and N. Kautsky, 1989. The role of ecosystems for sustainable development of aquaculture. Ambio, 18(4):234-43

Freire, J., L. Fernandez and E. Gonzalez-Gurrian, 1991. Influence of mussel raft culture on the diet of *Liocarcinus arcuatus* in the Ria de Arousa (Galicia, NW Spain). J.Shellfish Res., 9(1):45-57

Frid, C.L.J. and T.S. Mercer, 1989. Environmental monitoring of caged fishfarming in macrotidal environments. Mar.Pollut.Bull., 20(8):379-83

GESAMP (IMO/FAO/Unesco/WMO/WHO/IAEA/UN/UNEP Joint Group of Experts on the Scientific Aspects of Marine Pollution) 1980. Marine pollution implications of coastal area development. Rep.Stud.GESAMP, (11):114 p.

GESAMP (IMO/FAO/Unesco/WMO/WHO/IAEA/UN/UNEP Joint Group of Experts on the Scientific Aspects of Marine Pollution) 1986. Environmental Capacity. An approach to marine pollution prevention. Rep.Stud.GESAMP, (30):49 p.

GESAMP (IMO/FAO/Unesco/WMO/WHO/IAEA/UN/UNEP Joint Group of Experts on the Scientific Aspects of Marine Pollution) 1987. Land/sea boundary flux of contaminants: Contributions from rivers. Rep.Stud.GESAMP, (32):172 p.

GESAMP (IMO/FAO/Unesco/WMO/WHO/IAEA/UN/UNEP Joint Group of Experts on the Scientific Aspects of Marine Pollution) 1990a. Review of potentially harmful substances. Nutrients. Rep.Stud.GESAMP, (34):40 p.

GESAMP (IMO/FAO/Unesco/WMO/WHO/IAEA/UN/UNEP Joint Group of Experts on the Scientific Aspects of Marine Pollution) 1990b. The state of the marine environment. Rep.Stud.GESAMP, (39):112 p.

GESAMP (IMO/FAO/Unesco/WMO/WHO/IAEA/UN/UNEP Joint Group of Experts on the Scientific Aspects of Marine Pollution) 1991a. Coastal modelling. Rep.Stud.GESAMP, (43):192 p.

GESAMP (IMO/FAO/Unesco/WMO/WHO/IAEA/UN/UNEP Joint Group of Experts on the Scientific Aspects of Marine Pollution) 1991b. Global strategies for marine environmental protection. Rep.Stud.GESAMP, (45):36 p.

GESAMP (IMO/FAO/Unesco/WMO/WHO/IAEA/UN/UNEP Joint Group of Experts on the Scientific Aspects of Marine Pollution) 1991c. Reducing Environmental Impacts of Coastal Aquaculture. Rep.Stud.GESAMP, (47):35 p.

Gomez, E.D. *et al.*, 1990. State of the marine environment in the East Asian Seas Region. UNEP Reg.Seas Rep.Stud., (126):63 p.

Gowen, R.J. and N.B. Bradbury, 1987. The ecological impact of salmonid farming in coastal waters: A review. Oceanogr.Mar.Biol.Annu.Rev., 25:563-75

Gowen, R.J. and I.A. Ezzi, 1992. Assessment and prediction of the potential for hypernutrification and eutrophication associated with cage culture of salmonids in Scottish coastal waters. Natural Environment Research Council. Oban, Scotland, Dunstaffnage Marine Laboratory, 136 p. plus annexes.

Gowen, R.J., N.B. Bradbury and J.R. Brown, 1989. The use of simple models in assessing two of the interactions between fish farming and the marine environment. In Aquaculture - A biotechnology in progress. Proceedings of the International Conference Aquaculture Europe '87, held 2-5 June 1987 in Amsterdam, The Netherlands, edited by N. De Pauw, E. Jaspers, H. Ackefors and N. Wilkins. Bredene, European Aquaculture Society. Vol.2:1071-80

Gowen, R.J. *et al.*, 1988. Investigations into benthic enrichment, hypernutrification and eutrophication associated with mariculture in Scottish coastal waters (1984-1988). Stirling, University of Stirling, 290 p.

Gowen, R.J. *et al.*, 1990. Environmental impact of aquaculture activities. Eur.Aquacult.Soc.Spec.Publ., (12):257-83

Grave, K. *et al.*, 1990. Utilization of antibacterial drugs in salmonid farming in Norway during 1980-1988. Aquaculture, 86:347-58

Gray, J.S., A.D. McIntyre and J. Stirn, 1992. Manual of methods in aquatic environment research. Part 11: Biological assessment of marine pollution - with particular reference to benthos. FAO Fish.Tech.Pap., (324):49 p.

Gubbay, S., 1990. A future for the coast ? Proposals for a U.K. coastal zone management plan. A report for the World Wide Fund for Nature from the Marine Conservation Society. United Kingdom, 31 p.

Hakanson, I.. and M. Wallin, 1991. Use of ecometric analysis to establish load diagrams for nutrients in coastal areas. In Marine Aquaculture and Environment, edited by T. Makinen. Copenhagen, Nordic Council of Ministers. Nord 1991(22):9-23

Hakanson, L. *et al.*, 1988. Basic concepts concerning assessments of environmental effects of marine fish farms. Copenhagen, Nordic Council of Ministers. Nord 1988(90):103 p.

Halfon, E., 1989. Mathematical models for predicting the fate of contaminants in freshwater-ecosystems. In Aquatic ecotoxidology: fundamental concepts and methodologies, edited by A. Boudou and F. Ribeyre. Boca Raton, Florida, CRC Press. Vol. 2:257-74

Hellawell, J.M., 1986. Biological indicators of freshwater pollution and environmental management. (Pollution monitoring series). England, Elsevier Applied Science Publishers, 546 p.

Henderson, J.P. and N.R. Bromage, 1988. Optimising the removal of suspended solids from aquacultural effluents in settlement lakes. Aquacult.Eng., 7:167-81

Héral, M., 1991. Approches de la capacité trophique des écosystèmes conchylicoles: synthèse bibliographique. In The ecology and management aspects of extensive mariculture. A symposium held 20-23 June 1989 in Nantes, France, edited by S.J. Lockwood. Copenhagen, International Council for the Exploration of the Sea. ICES Mar.Sci.Symp., (192):48-62

Héral, M., J.M. Deslous-Paoli and J. Prout, 1986. Dynamique des productions et des biomasses des huîtres creuses cultivées (*Crassostrea angulata* et *Crassostrea gigas*) dans le bassin de Marennes-Oléron depuis un siècle. Copenhagen, International Council for the Exploration of the Sea, ICES CM F:41 p.

Hickmann, R.W., 1989. Farming the green mussel in New Zealand. World Aquacult., 20(4):20-8

Hildebrand, L.P., 1989. Canada's Experience with Coastal Zone Management. Halifax, The Oceans Institute of Canada, 118 p.

Hirono, Y. and S. van Eys, 1990. The Ecuadorian shrimp culture industry. INFOFISH Int., 4/90:53-8

Holmer, M., 1991. Impacts of aquaculture on surrounding sediments: generation of organic-rich sediments. Eur.Aquacult.Soc.Spec.Publ., (16)

Holmer, M. and E. Kristensen, 1992. Impact of marine fish cage farming on metabolism and sulfate reduction of underlying sediments. Mar.Ecol.Prog.Ser., 80:191-201

Honculada Primavera, J., 1991. Intensive prawn farming in the Philippines: ecological, social and economic impacts. Ambio, 20(1):28-33

Hopkins, T. A. and W. E. Manci, 1989. Feed conversion, waste and sustainable aquaculture. Aquacult.Mag., 15(2):30-6

Howarth, W., 1990. The law of aquaculture: the law relating to the farming of fish and shellfish in Britain. Oxford, Fishing News Books Ltd., 271 p.

Hufschmidt, M.M. *et al.*, 1983. Environment, natural systems and development. An economic valuation guide. Baltimore and London, The John Hopkins University Press, 327 p.

Huguenin, J.E. and J. Colt, 1989. Design and operating guide for aquaculture seawater systems. Dev.Aquacult.Fish.Sci., (20):264 p.

Huss, H.H., 1988. Fresh fish - quality and quality changes. A training manual prepared for the FAO/DANIDA training programme on fish technology and quality control. FAO Fish.Ser., (29):132 p.

Huss, H.H., 1991. Public health aspects of seafood consumption. INFOFISH Int., 3/91:27-32

Hwang, J., 1992. Taiwan: from success to uncertainty. Far East.Agricult., January/February 1992:18-21

ICES, 1990. Report of the Working Group on Environmental Impacts of Mariculture. International Council for the Exploration of the Sea. Mariculture Committee. C.M. 1990/F:12., 69 p.

Insull, D. and C.E. Nash, 1990. Aquaculture project formulation. FAO Fish.Tech.Pap., (316):129 p.

Ives, B.H., 1989. Pollution ! What's a farmer to do ? World Aquacult., 20(3):48-9

Iwama, G.K., 1991. Interactions between aquaculture and the environment. Crit.Rev.Environ.Control, 21(2):177-216

Jacobsen, P. and L. Berglind, 1988. Persistence of oxytetracycline in sediments from fish farms. Aquaculture, 70:365-70

Jensen, P., 1991. Aquafeeds: Reducing environmental impact. Feed Int., 12(8):6-12

Jernelov, A. and U. Marinov, 1990. An approach to environmental impact assessment for projects affecting the coastal and marine environment. UNEP, Nairobi. UNEP Reg.Seas Rep.Stud., (122):35 p.

Juhasz, F., 1991. An international comparison of sustainable coastal zone management policies. Proceedings of the International Conference on the Environmental Management of Enclosed Coastal Seas (EMECS'90) held 3-6 August 1990 in Kobe, Japan. Mar.Pollut.Bull., 23:595-602

Juliano, R.O., R. Guerrero (III) and I. Ronquillo, 1989. The introduction of exotic aquatic species in the Philippines. Asian Fish.Soc.Spec.Publ., (3):83-90

Kam, S.P., 1989. Application of remote sensing and geographical information systems in coastal area management. ICLARM Conf.Proc., (19):163-71

Kapetsky, J.M., 1982. Some potential environmental effects of coastal aquaculture with implications for site selection and aquaculture engineering. In Report of consultation:seminar on coastal fishpond engineering, held 4-12 August 1982 in Surabaya, Indonesia, edited by W.L. Chan, H.R. Rabanal and V. Soesanto. Manila, UNDP/FAO South China Sea Fisheries Development and Coordinating Programme. SCS/GEN/82/42, pp 76-82

Kapetsky, J.M., 1987a. Conversion of mangroves for pond aquaculture: some short-term and long-term remedies. FAO Fish.Rep., (370)Suppl.:129-41

Kapetsky, J.M., 1987b. Development of the mangrove ecosystem for forestry, fisheries and aquaculture. Symposium on ecosystem redevelopment: ecological, economic and social aspects, organized by Unesco and the Hungarian Academy of Sciences. Budapest, Hungary, 5-11 April 1987. Final Report, 10:31p.

Kapetsky J.M., L. McGregor and H. Nanne L., 1987. A geographical information system and satellite remote sensing to plan for aquaculture development: a FAO - UNEP/GRID cooperative study in Costa Rica. FAO Fish.Tech.Pap., (287):51 p.

Kaspar, H.F. *et al.*, 1985. Effects of mussel culture on the nitrogen cycle and benthic communities in Kenepru Sounds, New Zealand. Mar.Biol., 85:127-36

Kaspar, H.F., G.H. Hall and A.J. Holland, 1988. Effects of sea cage salmon farming on sediment nitrification and dissimilatory nitrate reductions. Aquaculture, 70:333-44

Katz, A., 1989. Coastal resource management in Belize: Potentials and problems. Ambio, 18(2):139-41

Kennedy, A.D., 1990. Marine reserve management in developing nations: Mida Creek - A case study from East Africa. Ocean Shoreline Manage., 14:105-32

Klaassen, G.A.J. and J.B. Opschoor 1991. Economics of sustainability or sustainability of economics: different paradigms. Ecol.Econ., 4:93-115

Könemann, H., 1981. Quantitative structure-activity relationships in fish toxicity studies. Part I: Relationship for 50 industrial pollutants. Toxicology, 19:209-21

Kontara, E.K., 1988. Shrimp culture management techniques. In Report of the training course on shrimp culture, held 2-19 December 1987 in Jepara, Indonesia. Manila, ASEAN/UNDP/FAO Regional small-scale coastal fisheries development project RAS/84/016. ASEAN/SF/88/GEN/3, pp 32-8

Kupka Hansen, P., K. Pittman and A. Ervik, 1991. Organic waste from marine fish farms - Effects on the seabed. In Marine Aquaculture and Environment, edited by T. Makinen. Copenhagen, Nordic Council of Ministers. Nord 1991(22):9-23

Landner, L., 1988. Hazardous chemicals in the environment - some new approaches to advanced assessment. Ambio, 17(6):360-6

Landner, L. (Editor), 1989. Chemicals in the Aquatic Environment: Advanced Hazard Assessment. Berlin, Springer, 416 p.

Larkin, P.A., 1991. Mariculture and fisheries: future prospects and partnerships. In The ecology and management aspects of extensive mariculture. A symposium held 20-23 June 1989 in Nantes, France, edited by S.J. Lockwood. Copenhagen, International Council for the Exploration of the Sea. ICES Mar.Sci.Symp., (192):6-14

Lauren-Maatta, C.A. *et al.*, 1991. Effects of fish farming on the macrobenthos of different bottom types. In Marine Aquaculture and Environment, edited by T. Makinen. Copenhagen, Nordic Council of Ministers. Nord 1991(22):57-83

Liao, I.C., 1989. *Penaeus monodon* culture in Taiwan: Through two decades of growth. Int.J.Aquac.Fish.Technol.,1:16-24

Lin, C.K., 1989. Prawn culture in Taiwan: What went wrong? World Aquacult., 20(2):19-21

Liu, C.I., 1989. Shrimp disease, prevention and treatment. In Proceedings of the Southeast Asia shrimp farm management workshop, held in the Philippines, Indonesia, Thailand. 26 July - 11 August 1989, edited by D.M. Akiyama. Singapore, American Soybean Association, pp 64-74

Llana, E.G., 1991. Production and utilisation of seaweeds in the Philippines. INFOFISH Int., 1/91:12-7

Lloyd, R., 1991a. Interpretation and application of ecotoxicological data: I. Single chemicals. In Ecotoxicology and the marine environment, edited by P.D. Abel and V. Axiak. New York, Ellis Horwood, pp 219-30

Lloyd, R., 1991b. Interpretation and application of ecotoxicological data: II. Complex effluents. In Ecotoxicology and the marine environment, edited by P.D. Abel and V. Axiak. New York, Ellis Horwood, pp 231-45

Lohani, B.N. and N. Halim, 1983. Recommended methodologies for rapid environmental impact assessment in developing countries: Experiences derived from cases studies in Thailand. In Environmental Impact Assessment for Developing Countries, edited by A.K. Biswas and Q. Geping. International Society for Ecological Modelling, United Nations University in Guangzhou, People's Republic of China and United Nations Environment Programme, pp 65-111

Lovatelli, A., 1990. Bivalves: status, problems and future in Asia. INFOFISH Int., 2/90:20-4

Lowry, K., 1989. Issues in designing a coastal management programme. ICLARM Conf.Proc., (19):191-204

Lumb, C.M., 1989. Self-pollution by Scottish salmon farms ? Mar.Pollut.Bull., 20(8):375-9

Maclean, J.L., 1989. Indo-Pacific Red Tides, 1985-1988. Mar.Pollut.Bull., 20(7):304-10

Maclean, J.L., 1991. Red tides and Asian seafarming. In Fish health management in Asia-Pacific. Report on a regional study and workshop on fish disease and fish health management. Bangkok, Network of Aquaculture Centres in Asia-Pacific. Asian Dev.Bank Agricult.Dep.Rep.Ser., (1):601-5

Mahmood, N., 1987. Effects of shrimp farming and other impacts on mangroves of Bangladesh. FAO Fish.Rep., (370)Suppl.:46-66

Maine, P.D. and C.E. Nash, 1987. Aquaculture sector development - A guideline for the preparation of a national plan. UNDP/FAO Aquaculture Development and Coordination Programme. Rome, FAO. ADCP/REP/87/27, 21 p.

Mäkinen, T., S. Lindgren and P. Eskelinen, 1988. Sieving as an effluent treatment method for aquaculture. Aquacult.Eng., 7:367-77

Matthes, H. and J.M. Kapetsky, 1988. Worldwide compendium of mangrove-associated aquatic species of economic importance. FAO Fish.Circ., (817):236 p.

McCoy, H.D., 1989. Commercial aquaculture zones. A legislative proposal. Aquacult.Mag., 15(6):39-46

McHenery, J.G., D. Saward and D.D. Seaton, 1991. Lethal and sub-lethal effects of the salmon de-lousing agent dichlorvos on the larvae of the lobster (*Homarus gammarus* L.) and herring (*Clupea harengus* L.). Aquaculture, 98:331-47

McManus, L.T. and T.E. Chua (Editcrs), 1990. The coastal environmental profile of Lingayen Gulf, Philippines. Manila, ASEAN/US Coastal Resources Management Project. Technical Publications Series No.5. ICLARM Tech.Rep., (22):69 p.

Meaden, G.J. and J.M. Kapetsky, 1991. Geographical information systems and remote sensing in inland fisheries and aquaculture. FAO Fish.Tech.Pap., (318):262 p.

Mena Millar, A., 1989. La explotación del camarón en América Latina y el Caribe. FAO Circ.Pesca, (820):30 p.

Menasveta, P., 1987. Effects of water pollution on aquaculture development in Thailand. Water Qual.Bull., 12(3):116-29

Merschrod, K., 1989. In search of a strategy for coastal zone management in the Thirld World: Notes from Ecuador. Coast.Manage., 17:63-74

Meyer, F.P. and R.A. Schnick, 1989. A review of chemicals used for the control of fish diseases. Rev.Aquat.Sci., 1(4):693-710

Mok, T.K., 1982. The environmental impact of cage culture operations. In Report of the training course on small-scale pen and cage culture for finfish, held October 1981 in Laguna, Philippines, and 1-13 November 1981 in Aberdeen, Hong Kong, edited by R.D. Guerrero III and V. Soesanto. Manila, UNDP/FAO South China Sea Fisheries Development and Coordinating Programme. SCS/GEN/82/34, pp 129-31

Molnar, J.J. and B.L. Duncan, 1989. Monitoring and evaluating aquacultural projects. In Monitoring and evaluating the impacts of small-scale fishery projects, edited by R.B. Pollnac. Kingston, RI, International Center for Marine Resource Development at the University of Rhode Island, pp 28-40

Moore, J.W. and S. Ramamoorthy, 1984. Heavy metals in natural waters: applied monitoring and impact assessment. New York, Springer, 269 p.

Muir, J.F., 1982. Economic aspects of waste treatment in fish culture. EIFAC Tech.Pap., (41):123-35

Muir, J.F. and D.J. Baird, 1991. Environmental management of aquaculture development in Cyprus. Report of FAO project TCP/CYP/9152. Rome, FAO, 64 p. plus annexes.

NACA, 1989. Report of the workshop and study tour on mollusc sanitation and marketing; 15-28 October 1989, France. UNDP/FAO Rergional seafarming development and demonstration project (RAS/86/024). Bangkok, Network of Aquaculture Centres in Asia, 212 p.

Nash, C.E. (Editor), 1991. Production of aquatic animals: crustaceans, molluscs, amphibians and reptiles. Amsterdam, Elsevier. World Animal Science: C4, 244 p.

Nath Roy, R. (Editor), 1984. Consultation on social feasibility of coastal aquaculture; held 26 November - 01 December 1984 in Madras, India. Organized by National Swedish Board of Fisheries and Bay of Bengal Programme (FAO/SIDA). BOBP/MIS/2: 125 p.

NCC, 1989. Fishfarming and the safeguard of the natural marine environment of Scotland. The Nature Conservancy Council. Based on a report by the Institute of Aquaculture, University of Stirling, 136 p.

Neal, R.A., 1984. Aquaculture expansion and environmental considerations. Mazingira, 8(3):24-8

New, M.B., 1987. Feed and feeding of fish and shrimp - a manual on the preparation and presentation of compound feeds for shrimp and fish in aquaculture. Rome, FAO. ADCP/REP/87/26, 275 p.

New, M.B., 1989. Formulated aquaculture feeds in Asia: Some thoughts on comparative economics, industrial potential, problems and resrearch needs in relation to the small-scale farmer. In Report of the workshop on shrimp and finfish feed development, held 25-29 October 1988 in Johore Bahru, Malaysia. Manila, ASEAN/UNDP/FAO Regional Small-Scale Coastal Fisheries Development Project. ASEAN/SF/89/GEN/11, pp. 19-30

New, M.B., 1990a. Shrimp farming experiences environmental problems. Brussels, Commission of the European Communities. EC Fish.Coop.Bull., 3(3):4-6

New, M.B., 1990b. Compound feedstuffs for shrimp culture. In Technical and economic aspects of shrimp farming. Proceedings of the AQUATECH'90 Conference, Kuala Lumpur, Malaysia, 11-14 June 1990, edited by M.B. New, H. de Saram and T. Singh. Organized by Infofish in collaboration with the Fisheries Development Authority of Malaysia, pp 79-118

New, M.B., 1991. Turn of the millenium aquaculture: Navigating troubled waters or riding the crest of the wave ? World Aquacult., 22(3):28-49

New, M.B. and U.N. Wijkstrom, 1990. Feed for thought - Some observations on aquaculture feed production in Asia. World Aquacult., 20(1):17-23

O'Connor, B.D.S. *et al.*, 1989. The use of REMOTS technology in monitoring coastal enrichment resulting from mariculture. Mar.Pollut.Bull., 20(8):384-90

ODA, 1988. Manual of environmental appraisal. London, Overseas Development Administration, 97 p.

Okaichi, T., 1991. Toxic phytoplankton - Human health and aquatic animal health significance. In Fish health management in Asia-Pacific. Report on a regional study and workshop on fish disease and fish health management. Bangkok, Network of Aquaculture Centres in Asia-Pacific. Asian Dev.Bank Agricult.Dep.Rep.Ser., (1):525-34

Otwell, W.S., G.E. Rodrick and R.E. Martin (Editors), 1991. Molluscan shellfish depuration. Boca Raton, Florida, CRC Press, 384 p.

Padlan, P.G., 1982. Pond culture of fish, shrimps and crabs in intertidal zones in the Far East. CIFA Tech.Pap., (9):187-204

Paw, J.N., S. Bunpapong, A.T. White and M.S.M. Sadorra (Editors), 1988. The coastal environmental profile of Ban Don Bay and Phangnga Bay, Thailand. Manila, ASEAN/US Coastal Resources Management Project. Technical Publications Series No.2. ICLARM Tech.Rep., (20):78 p.

Pedersen, T.N. *et al.*, 1988. LENKA - A nation-wide analysis of the suitability of the Norwegian coast and watercourses for aquaculture. A coastal zone management programme. Copenhagen, International Council for the Exploration of the Sea. ICES C.M. 1988/F:11, 18 p.

Pedini, M., 1981. Penaeid shrimp culture in tropical developing countries. FAO Fish.Circ., (732):14 p.

Perez Camacho, A., R. Gonzalez and J. Fuentes, 1991. Mussel culture in Galicia (N.W. Spain). Aquaculture, (94):263-78

Petit, J. and P. Maurel, 1983. L'épuration des eaux en pisciculture d'eau douce: ses méthodes à travers le monde. Piscic.Fr., 72:21-30

Phillips, D.J.H. and S. Tanabe, 1989. Aquatic pollution in the Far East. Mar.Pollut.Bull., 20(7):297-303

Phillips, M.J. 1990. Environmental aspects of seaweed culture. In Regional workshop on the culture and utilization of seaweeds, held 27-31 August 1990 in Cebu City, The Philippines. Bangkok, Regional Seafarming Development and Demonstration Project RAS/90/002 and Network of Aquaculture Centres in Asia (NACA). Technical resource papers: Vol. 2:51-62

Phillips, M.J., Beveridge, M.C.M. and R.M. Clarke, 1991. Impact of aquaculture on water resources. In Aquaculture and water quality, edited by D.E. Brune and J.R. Tomasso. Baton Rouge, World Aquaculture Society. Adv.World Aquacult., (3):568-91

Phillips, M.J., Lin, C.K. and M.C.M. Beveridge, (in press). Shrimp culture and the environment - Lessons from the world's most rapidly expanding warm water aquaculture sector. Contribution to the ICLARM Conference on Environment and Third World Aquaculture Development. Bellagio, Italy, 17-22 September 1990. Manila, International Center for Living Aquatic Resources Management.

Piedrahita, R.H. and P. Giovannini, 1991. Fertilized non-fed pond systems. In Aquaculture Systems Engineering. Proceedings of the World Aquaculture Society and the American Society of Agricultural Engineers: A jointly sponsored session. WAS 22nd Annual Meeting, 16-20 June 1991, San Juan, Puerto Rico. ASAE publication 02-91, pp 1-14

Pierce, D., 1988. Economists befriend the earth. New Scient., 120(1639):34-39

Pillay, T.V.R., 1990. Aquaculture: principles and practices. Oxford, Fishing News Books, Blackwell, 575 p.

Pillay, T.V.R., 1992. Aquaculture and the Environment. Oxford, Fishing News Books, Blackwell, 189 p.

Piotrowski, J.K. and M.J. Inskip, 1981. Health effects of methylmercury. Monitoring and Assessment Research Centre, Chelsea College. University of London. MARC Tech.Rep., (24):82 p.

Poernomo, A., 1990. Site selection for coastal shrimp ponds. In Technical and economic aspects of shrimp farming. Proceedings of the AQUATECH'90 Conference, Kuala Lumpur, Malaysia, 11-14 June 1990, edited by M.B. New, H. de Saram and T. Singh. Organized by Infofish in collaboration with the Fisheries Development Authority of Malaysia, pp 3-23

Poernomo, A. and V.P. Singh, 1982. Problems, field identification and practical solutions of acid sulfate soils for brackishwater fishponds. In Report of consultation:seminar on coastal fishpond engineering, held 4-12 August 1982 in Surabaya, Indonesia, edited by W.L. Chan, H.R. Rabanal and V. Soesanto. Manila, UNDP/FAO South China Sea Fisheries Development and Coordinating Programme. SCS/GEN/82/42, pp 49-61

Porter, C.B., P. Krost and H. Gordin, (in press). Cage culture of gilthead seabream (*Sparus aurata*): Reduction of organic matter accumulation by use of grey mullet (*Mugil cephalus*). Eur.Aquacult.Soc.Spec.Publ., (16)

Pravdic, V., 1987. Environmental capacity: An approach for prevention of water pollution. Water Qual.Bull., 12(4):137-66

Pullin, R.S.V., 1989. Third World aquaculture and the environment. NAGA ICLARM Quarterly, 12(1):10-3

Quincy, D., 1990. Réglementation et pollution piscicole. Le vent du Nord? Aqua Rev., 32:7-9

Rodhouse, P.G. *et al.*, 1985. Production of mussels, *Mytilus edulis*, in suspended culture and estimates of carbon and nitrogen flow: Killary Harbour, Ireland. J.Biol.Assoc.U.K., 65:55-68

Rosenberry, B. (Editor), 1990. World shrimp farming 1990. San Diego, Aquaculture Digest, 40 p.

Rosenthal, H., *et al.*, 1988. Report of the *ad hoc* study group on environmental impact of mariculture. Copenhagen, ICES Coop.Res.Rep., (154):83 p.

Rueness, J., 1989. *Sargassum muticum* and other introduced Japanese macroalgae: biological pollution of European coasts. Mar.Pollut.Bull., 20(4):173-6

Ruying, S. and W. Qingyin, 1992. Laminaria culture in China. INFOFISH Int., 1/92:40-3

Saclauso, C.A., 1989. Brackish water aquaculture: threat to the environment ? NAGA ICLARM Quarterly, 12(3):6-8

Samuelsen, O.B., 1989. Degradation of oxytetracycline in seawater at two different temperatures and light intensities, and the persistence of oxytetracycline in the sediment of a fish farm. Aquaculture, 83:7-16

Santelices, B. and M.S. Doty, 1989. A review of Gracilaria farming. Aquaculture, 78:95-133

Schmidt, U.W., 1982. Selected socio-economic aspects of coastal aquaculture in tropical regions with respect to planning and implementation. CIFA Tech.Pap., (9):129-41

Schnick, R., 1991. Chemicals for worldwide aquaculture. In Fish health management in Asia-Pacific. Report on a regional study and workshop on fish disease and fish health management. Bangkok, Network of Aquaculture Centres in Asia-Pacific. Asian Dev.Bank Agricult.Dep.Rep.Ser., (1):441-67

Schnick, R.A., F.P. Meyer and D.L. Gray, 1989. A guide to approved chemicals in fish production and fishery resources management. Little Rock, Arkansas, U.S. Fish and Wildlife Service and University of Arkansas Cooperative Extension Service. MP241-5M-3-89RV, 27 p.

Sen Gupta, R. *et al.*, 1990. State of the marine environment in the South Asian Seas Region. UNEP Reg.Seas Rep.Stud.,(123):42 p.

Seymour, E.A. and A. Bergheim, 1991. Towards a reduction of pollution from intensive aquaculture with reference to farming of salmonids in Norway. Aquacult.Eng., 10:73-88

Shang, Y.C., 1990. Socioeconomic constraints of aquaculture in Asia. World Aquacult., 21(1):34-43

Shariff, M. and R. Subasinghe, 1990. Health aspects of Asian aquaculture. INFOFISH Int., 5/90:35-8

Shopley, J.B. and R.F. Fuggle, 1984. A comprehensive review of current environmental impact assessment methods and techniques. J.Environ.Manage., 18:25-47

Shpigel, M. and R. Fridman, 1990. Propagation of the Manila clam (*Tapes semidecussatus*) in the effluent of fish aquaculture ponds in Eilat, Israel. Aquaculture, 90:113-22

Shumway, S.E., 1989. Toxic algae: A serious threat to shellfish aquaculture. World Aquacult., 20(4):65-74

Shumway, S.E., 1990. A review of the effects of algal blooms on shellfish and aquaculture. J.World Aquacult.Soc., 21(2):65-103

Shuval, I.H., 1986. Thalassogenic diseases. Nairobi, UNEP. UNEP Reg.Seas Rep.Stud., (79):44 p.

Silas, E.G., 1987. Management of mangrove associated fisheries and aquaculture in the Sunderbans, India. FAO Fish.Rep., (370)Suppl.:21-43

Silvert, W., (in press). Assessing environmental impacts of finfish aquaculture in marine waters. To be printed in Aquaculture.

Simpson, H.J. and M. Pedini, 1985. Brackishwater aquaculture in the tropics: the problem of acid sulphate soils. FAO Fish.Circ., (791):32 p.

Simpson, H.J. and M. Pedini, 1987. Acidity impacts on brackish-water aquaculture. Water Qual.Bull., 12(4):145-67

Sin, O.K., L.P. Chong and H. Hanafi, 1989. Prawn / shrimp culture in Malaysia. Kuala Lumpur, Department of Fisheries, Ministry of Agriculture, Malaysia.

Sindermann, C.J., 1986. Strategies for reducing risks from introductions of aquatic organisms: A marine perspective. Fisheries, 11(2):10-5

Singh, V.P., 1987. Reclamation of fishponds in acid sulphate soils. Water Qual.Bull., 12(4):159-62

Sitoy, H.S., 1988. Farming of mussels and oysters. In Perspectives in aquaculture development in Southeast Asia and Japan. Proceedings of the seminar on aquaculture development in Southeast Asia, held 8-12 September 1987 in Iloilo City, Philippines, edited by J.B. Juario and L.B. Benitez. Tigbauan, Iloilo, Southeast Asian Fisheries Development Center, pp 231-48

Smaal, A.C., 1991. The ecology and cultivation of mussels: new advances. Aquaculture, 94:245-61

Smith, I.R. and R. Pestano-Smith, 1985. Social feasibility of coastal aquaculture. ICLARM Newsl., 8(3):6-8

Soemodihardjo, S. and I. Soerianegara, 1989. Country report: Indonesia. The status of mangrove forests in Indonesia. In Symposium on mangrove management: Its ecological and economic considerations, held in Bogor, Indonesia, 9-11 August, 1988. Bogor, Southeast Asian Regional Center for Tropical Biology (SEAMEO - BIOTROP). BIOTROP Spec.Publ., (37):73-114

Sorensen, J.C. and S.T. McCreary, 1990. Institutional arrangements for managing of coastal resources and environments. Washington, D.C., National Park Service, US Dept. of the Interior and US Agency for International Development. Renewable resources information series; Coastal management publication No.1, revised second edition, 194 p.

Stansell, J., 1992. Fear and loathing close a fish farm in Cyprus. New Scient., 133(1812):14

Stickney, R.R., 1990. A global overview of aquaculture production. Food Rev.Int., 6(3):299-315

Sunaryanto, A., 1988. An outline of discussion on pests and diseases of shrimps. In Report of the training course on shrimp culture, held 2-19 December 1987 in Jepara, Indonesia. Manila, ASEAN/UNDP/FAO Regional small-scale coastal fisheries development project RAS/84/016. ASEAN/SF/88/GEN/3, pp 39-44

Sweden, 1983. The environmental impact of aquaculture. Stockholm, Swedish Council for Planning and Coordination of Research. Report 83:5, 74 p.

Tacon, A.G.J., 1987a. The nutrition and feeding of farmed fish and shrimp - a training manual. 1. The essential nutrients. Brasilia, FAO. GCP/RLA/075/ITA Field Document 2, 117 p.

Tacon, A.G.J., 1987b. The nutrition and feeding of farmed fish and shrimp - a training manual. 2. Nutrient sources and composition. Brasilia, FAO. GCP/RLA/075/ITA Field Document 5, 129 p.

Tacon, A.G.J., 1988. The nutrition and feeding of farmed fish and shrimp - a training manual. 3. Feeding methods. Brasilia, FAO. GCP/RLA/075/ITA Field Document 7, 208 p.

Tacon, A.G.J., (in press). Aquaculture nutrition and feeding in developing countries: A practical approach to research and development. In: Proceedings of IV International Symposium on Fish Nutrition and Feeding, held 24-27 June 1991 in Biarritz, France.

Terchunian, A. *et al.*, 1986. Mangrove mapping in Ecuador: the impact of shrimp pond construction. Environ.Manage., 10(3):345-50

Thorhaug, A., 1987. Restoration of mangroves and seagrasses and attendant economic benefits for fisheries and aquaculture: management, policy and planning. FAO Fish.Rep., (370)Suppl.:142-59

Thorhaug, A., 1990. Restoration of mangroves and seagrasses - Economic benefits for fisheries and mariculture. In Environmental Restoration. Science and Strategies for Restoring the Earth, edited by J.J. Berger. Washington, D.C., Island Press, pp 265-81

Thrower, S.J., 1990. Shellfish depuration. INFOFISH Int., 5/90:48-51

Ti, T.L., R. Hassan and L.D. Rajamanickam, 1982. Coastal mangrove swamps for fishponds: A focus on some environmental factors. In Report of consultation:seminar on coastal fishpond engineering, held 4-12 August 1982 in Surabaya, Indonesia, edited by W.L. Chan, H.R. Rabanal and V. Soesanto. Manila, UNDP/FAO South China Sea Fisheries Development and Coordinating Programme. SCS/GEN/82/42, pp 62-71

Tookwinas, S., 1990. Pen culture techniques of marine shrimp in Thailand. INFOFISH Int., 2/90:38-40

Trono, G.C.Jr., 1986. Seaweed culture in the Asia-Pacific region. Bangkok, FAO/Regional Office for Asia and the Pacific. RAPA Publication 1987/3, 41 p.

Trono, G.C.Jr., 1990. A review of the production technologies of tropical species of economic seaweeds. In Regional workshop on the culture and utilization of seaweeds, held 27-31 August 1990 in Cebu City, The Philippines. Bangkok, Regional Seafarming Development and Demonstration Project RAS/90/002 and Network of Aquaculture Centres in Asia (NACA). Technical resource papers: Vol.2:3-26

Tseng, C.K., 1987. Laminaria mariculture in China. FAO Fish.Tech.Pap., (281): 239-64

Turner, G.E., 1988. Codes of practice and manual of procedures for consideration of introductions and transfers of marine and freshwater organisms. EIFAC Occ.Pap., (23):44 p.

Turrel, W.R. and A.L.S. Munro, 1989. Sea cage culture of atlantic salmon: model study on the fate of soluble wastes. In Aquaculture. A review of recent experience. Paris, Organisation for Economic Co-operation and Development (OECD), pp 92-104

UNDP, 1991. Handbook and guidelines for environmental management and sustainable development. New York, United Nations Development Programme, 55 p. plus annexes.

UNDP/FAO, 1989. Culture of Kelp (*Laminaria japonica*) in China. Manual prepared for the *Laminaria* polyculture with mollusc training course, held 15 June - 31 July 1989 in Qingdao, China. Bangkok, Rome, FAO. Regional seafarming development and demonstration project (RAS/86/024). Training Manual 89/5, 204 p.

UNDP/Norway/FAO, 1987. Thematic evaluation of aquaculture. Rome, FAO, 85 p. plus annexes.

UNEP, 1988. Environmental Impact Assessment. Basic procedures for developing countries. Bangkok, United Nations Environment Programme (UNEP) Regional Office for Asia and the Pacific, 16 p.

UNEP, 1990a. Environmental guidelines for fish farming. Nairobi, UNEP. Environ.Manage.Guidel., (19): 50 p.

UNEP, 1990b. Technical annexes to the report on the state of the marine environment. UNEP Reg.Seas Rep.Stud., 114/1 and 114/2: 676 p.

Van Houtte, A.R., N. Bonucci and W.R. Edeson, 1989. A preliminary review of selected legislation governing aquaculture. Rome, FAO. ADCP/REP/89/42, 81 p.

Viarengo, A. and L. Canesi, 1991. Mussels as biological indicators of pollution. Aquaculture, 94:225-43

Walford,J. and T.J. Lam, 1987. Floating hatchery and net gage culture of *Penaeus indicus* in the Straits of Johore, Singapore. Aquaculture, 67:11-32

Wallin, M. and L. Hakanson, 1991. Nutrient loading models for estimating the environmental effects of marine fish farms. In Marine Aquaculture and Environment, edited by T. Makinen. Copenhagen, Nordic Council of Ministers. Nord 1991(22):39-55

Wang, J.K., 1990. Managing shrimp pond water to reduce discharge problems. Aquacult.Eng., 9:61-73

Warrer-Hansen, I., 1982. Methods of treatment of waste water from trout farming. EIFAC Tech.Pap., (41):133-21

Weston, D.P., 1990. Qualitative examination of macrobenthic community changes along an organic enrichment gradient. Mar.Ecol.Prog.Ser., 61:233-44

Weston, D.P., 1991. The effects of aquaculture on indigenous biota. In Aquaculture and water quality, edited by D.E. Brune and J.R. Tomasso. Baton Rouge, World Aquaculture Society. Adv.World Aquacult., (3):534-67

Weston, D.P. and R.J. Gowen, 1988. Assessment and prediction of the effects of salmon net-pen culture on the benthic environment. Seattle, Washington, Dept. of Fisheries. Technical report 414; Ref.: M88-2, 62 p.

White, A.T., P. Martosubroto and M.S.M. Sadorra (Editors), 1989. The coastal environmental profile of Segara Anakan-Cilcap, South Java, Indonesia. Manila, ASEAN/US Coastal Resources Management Project. Technical Publications Series No.4. ICLARM Tech.Rep., (25):82 p.

WHO, 1984. Aquatic (marine and freshwater) biotoxins. WHO Environ.Health Crit., (37):95 p.

WHO Expert Committee, 1974. Fish and shellfish hygiene. Rome, FAO and Geneva, World Health Organisation, PM/E8465:62 p. and WHO Tech.Rep.Ser., (550):62 p.

Wickins, J.F., 1986. Prawn farming today: opportunities, techniques and developments. Outlook Agricult., 15:52-60

Williams, R.R. and D.V. Lightner, 1988. Regulatory status of therapeutants for penaeid shrimp culture in the United States. J.World Aquacult.Soc., 19(4):188-96

Wu, C.Y., 1990. Cultivation of temperate seaweeds in the Asia-Pacific region. In Regional workshop on the culture and utilization of seaweeds, held 27-31 August 1990 in Cebu City, The Philippines. Bangkok, Regional Seafarming Development and Demonstration Project RAS/90/002 and Network of Aquaculture Centres in Asia (NACA). Technical resource papers: Vol. 2:27-32

Yap, W.G., 1990. Backyard hatcheries take off in Jepara. INFOFISH Int., 2/90:42-7

Zamora, P.M., 1989. Country report: The Philippines. Mangroves of the Philippines. In Symposium on mangrove management: Its ecological and economic considerations, held in Bogor, Indonesia, 9-11 August, 1988. Bogor, Southeast Asian Regional Center for Tropical Biology (SEAMEO - BIOTROP). BIOTROP Spec.Publ., (37):43-65

Anonymus, 1990. Farms save money using wrasse to clear lice. Fish Farming Int., 17(8):52-3

ANNEX 1

A short case study

ASIA

# PRAWN CULTURE IN TAIWAN

## What went wrong?

*by C. Kwei Lin*

**In 1987, Taiwan produced 80,000 mt of *Penaeus monodon*. A year later the industry collapsed to 20,000 mt because of the onslaught of virulent diseases. It now appears that these diseases were a direct result of ecosystem mismanagement resulting from poor farming practices, and that the disaster should be considered a model for aquatic farmers everywhere.**

Taiwan was once known as the "Mecca of Black Tiger Prawn Aquaculture." Production of farmed shrimp (*Penaeus monodon*) increased from a few thousand tonnes in the early 1980s to 80,000 tonnes in 1987. Like many other developing aquaculture ventures, black tiger prawn farming in Taiwan grew rapidly and then collapsed. In 1988, production dropped to less than 20,000 tonnes, 25% of the 1987 level, due to a disease caused by *Monodon baculovirus* (MBV) that struck prawns on 40-80% of the farms throughout the island.

In retrospect, it appears that the unprecedented increase in production doomed the shrimp industry in Taiwan. The expanding industry mobilized virtually all available resources on the island and directed them toward shrimp culture: suitable coastal land, salt and freshwater supply, formulated feeds, spawners and seed production, and trained personnel. Expansion soon exceeded the carrying capacity of existing resources, and environmental deterioration commenced. This resulted from pollution from shrimp farms as well as from the heavy industry that is concentrated in the region. This report summarizes the underlying causes of mass mortality of shrimp on farms in Taiwan during 1988.

## Causes

*Larval Rearing Conditions.*

Under normal conditions healthy larvae are produced by the first couple of spawns from naturally matured spawners, and larval development to postlarva takes approximately 24 days at a water temperature of 28°C. However, the rapid expansion of shrimp culture during the 1980s caused a dramatic increase in demand for shrimp seedstock, which prompted the seedstock producers to use multiple spawnings and increase the rearing temperature to as high as 35°C to enhance larval development and growth and reduce the rearing period by about 7 days. In addition, a variety of antibiotics and nutritional additives were applied to increase the larval survival rate from the usual 30% to as much as 70-90%. The larvae reared under such intensive conditions in an almost sterile environment had little resistance to latent pathogens and readily succumbed to diseases.

*Pond Aging*

The carrying capacity of shrimp ponds decreases with use because of the accumulation of organic matter in the mud on the bottom of the pond. The heavy use of ground water in most Taiwanese shrimp ponds may have increased the intrusion of organic matter into the deeper layers of the substrate, making it difficult to remove by ordinary leaching or scraping of the pond bottom. Water quality deteriorates rapidly when the substrate conditions are poor.

*Over stocking*

The normal stocking density for tiger prawns in intensive pond culture is 20-30 shrimp/m$^2$, but in the last two years it has been increased to 60, 80, even 100 shrimp/m$^2$. Such high density stresses the shrimp, enhances pond aging due to low feed conversion efficiency, and increases the probability of disease.

**The use of drugs in shrimp aquaculture was widespread**

*Feed Quality*

Shrimp feed production increased from 800 tonnes by 3 producers in 1978 to 100,000 tonnes by 56 producers in 1986. Although the general quality of formulated shrimp feed improved, it was inconsistent, and the use of antibiotics by the shrimp farmers was considered problematical. In addition, many of the feed products and additives on the market were unregistered.

*Drugs*

The use of chemicals in shrimp aquaculture was widespread because no legal registration was required for their use. Furthermore, most drug distributors were trained as livestock veterinarians, unable to provide advice on the use of drugs on aquatic animals. Vendors who sold drugs to farmers were even less aware of the chemical implications, and this abuse of drugs damaged shrimp health and water quality, and increased the resistance of pathogens to antibiotics.

> **Pathogens were transmitted rapidly along the coast from one farm to another.**

*Water Pollution*

In recent years the coastal water in Taiwan has become seriously polluted by industrial wastes, particularly organic chemicals and heavy metals, which are highly toxic to shrimp. In addition, waste water rich in organic and phytoplankton nutrients has been discharged at will into the public waters which also served as the source of seawater for the ponds. Although farmers were prudent in site selection and secured their own sources of water, little attention was paid to the public waterways that received the discharge from the farms. This waste water, which included diseased shrimp, fish and refuse, was distributed along the coast in the vicinity of the water intakes for the shrimp farms, and pathogens were therefore transmitted rapidly from one farm to another.

*Inexperience*

No licenses or special qualifications are required for shrimp farming, so many growers who were attracted by the profit potential lacked the necessary knowledge for shrimp culture. Inappropriate husbandry practices combined with unsound advice resulted in an unbalanced pond environment and poor shrimp growth, and growers caught in that situation were often willing to try anything that might remedy their problems.

## Diseases

Viral, bacterial and protozoal infections are causing mortality among Taiwanese farmed shrimp. *Monodon baculovirus* (MBV) is a viral disease that is most common (80%) in juvenile shrimp and was responsible for the recent mass shrimp mortality in pond culture.

In addition, bacterial infections of the hepatopancreas are caused by species of the *Vibrio* bacterium, including *Vibrio vulnificus, V. flavialis,* and *V. alginolyticus*. There are also external bacterial and protozoa infections, and a combination of external protozoa and bacteria in the hepatopancreas.

## Recommendations

As a result of their investigations into the causes of shrimp mortality, Taiwanese scientists have made the following recommendations to the shrimp farmers and to the government:

*To shrimp Farmers:*

- Be thorough in the preparation of ponds, including the drying and removal of aged bottom soils;
- Select healthy seedstock and avoid those that are raised at a temperature higher than 32°C;
- Introduce rigid control over the use of drugs in the hatcheries;
- Stock post larvae into the ponds during the early morning or evening and keep the stocking density below $30/m^2$;
- Maintain good water quality and a healthful pond bottom by using a carefully monitored feeding regime;
- Use a feeding net to observe shrimp feeding behavior and health. If the shrimp show signs of abnormality or disease, consult with experts before applying drugs;
- Eliminate MBV infections by improving water and bottom quality and increasing protein content in the diet;
- If MBV infection occurs, prevent its spread by collecting and burning infected shrimp and sterilizing pond water before it is discharged;
- Assist in documenting disease information by reporting and discussing disease occurrences with local fisheries officers;
- Diversify pond culture by including finfish, clams and other species of shellfish.

*To Government and the Public:*

- Legislate stricter regulations governing aquaculture in order to prevent irresponsible practices;
- Require registration and an operational license for all commercial farms, including on-farm certification by the government;
- Upgrade the qualifications and capability of personnel in public research institutions and local extension systems involved in fish disease work;
- Legislate a pharmaceutical policy pertaining to aquacultural applications, including legal punishment for violators;
- Modernize aquacultural infrastructures to facilitate management and supervision of shrimp farms;
- Try to minimize the damage to aquaculture morale that is caused by inaccurate or irresponsible reporting by the public media;
- Improve the quality of extension services;
- Provide assistance and supervision to the commercial feed producers to ensure that they maintain feed quality and market responsibility.

## Conclusions

The mass mortality among black tiger prawns caused by virulent diseases in Taiwan was unprecedented in intensive shrimp aquaculture. Analysis of the fundamental causes of the diseases revealed that most of the factors were man-made and could be averted. It is essential that hi-tech aquaculture systems be regarded as an integral part of the natural environment and that their quality be ensured. The disastrous experiences of the Taiwanese shrimp farmers was a valuable lesson for shrimp farmers, related industries and government officials in Taiwan and elsewhere in the world.

---

*C. Kwei Lin is with the Agricultural and Food Engineering Division, Asian Institute of Technology, P.O. Box 2754, Bangkok, Thailand.* ♦

## ANNEX 2

Multiple uses of coastal resources: potential environmental changes and impacts of social concern (modified from Sorensen and McCreary, 1990).

Note: this table is only an indicative list of sketchily described impact chains, and is <u>not</u> intended to explain cause and effect elationships.

| USE OR ACTIVITY ——— ——— ⟶ | ENVIRONMENTAL CHANGE ——— ⟶ | IMPACT OF SOCIAL CONCERN |
|---|---|---|
| <u>A. Estuary, harbor and inshore water quality impacts</u> | | |
| domestic and industrial sewage and waste disposal | estuary pollution, particularly adjacent to urban areas | decreased fish yields, contamination of fish, shellfish and water contact areas |
| tourism sewage disposal | estuary pollution | decreased fish yields |
| domestic and/or tourism sewage disposal | estuary and beach pollution | decreased tourism and recreation attraction |
| flood control and/or agricultural development, impoundments or diversions of coastal rivers | increased estuary salinity, decreased estuary circulation | decreased field yields |
| coastal oil development, chronic release of oil and/or large oil spills from accidents | oil pollution of estuarine and inshore waters | decreased fish yields, tainted fish and shellfish, decreased recreation or tourism quality |
| port development and shipping and/or offshore shipping of oil, chronic release of oil and/or large oil spills from accidents | oil pollution of estuarine and inshore waters | decreased fish yields, decreased recreation or tourism quality |
| agricultural pesticides | toxic pollution of estuaries and inshore waters | decreased fish yields, fish kills |

| USE OR ACTIVITY ——— ——— ⟶ | ENVIRONMENTAL CHANGE ——— ⟶ | IMPACT OF SOCIAL CONCERN |
|---|---|---|
| agricultural development and fertilizer | increased amount of nutrients entering estuaries, eutrophication, pollution | decreased fish yields, fish kills |
| crop, grazing, mining or forestry practices in coastal watersheds | watershed erosion, estuary sedimentation and increased turbidity, watershed erosion, floodplain deposition | decreased fish yieds, increased flood hazard |
| crop, grazing or forestry practices in coastal watersheds | watershed erosion, increased sedimentation, changed deposition of sedimens in bays, deltas and inshore waters | beaches covered with unattractive sediment, decreased recreation and tourism attraction |
| crop, grazing or forestry practices in coastal watersheds and inshore areas | watershed erosion, increased sedimentation of bays, deltas, and port areas | sedimentation of navigation channels and berths |
| coastal mining | increased sedimentation and turbidity, change in composition of bottom sediments | decreased fish yields |
| <u>B. Groundwater quality and quantity</u> | | |
| agricultural development, tourism and residential development | withdrawal of groundwater at rate greater than natural recharge, salt water intrusion of aquifer | contamination of groundwater for domestic and/or agricultural use |
| <u>C. Filling of wetlands (including mangroves)</u> | | |
| port development | filling of wetlands | decreased fish yields |
| port development | filling of wetlands | decreased fishing or mariculture areas |
| mining and soil disposal, tourism development, residential development | filling of wetlands | decreased fish yields |

| USE OR ACTIVITY ——— ——— ⟶ | ENVIRONMENTAL CHANGE ——— ⟶ | IMPACT OF SOCIAL CONCERN |
|---|---|---|
| D. Mangrove impacts | | |
| agricultural, maricultural or salt evaporation development | draining or diking of mangroves | decreased fish yields, reduction or loss of rare or endangered species |
| mangrove harvesting for wood chips, fuelwood and building materials | harvesting at rate greater than sustainable yields, decreased productivity | decreased fish yields, decreased timber yield of successive harvests |
| mangrove harvesting for wood chips, fuelwood and building materials | harvesting at rate greater than sustainable yield, loss of habitat | reduction or loss of rare or endangered species |
| nining (usually tin) | local removal of mangrove forest | decreased fish yields |
| :. Coral reef and atoll impacts | | |
| nunicipal and/or industrial sewage disposal | coral reef pollution | decreased fish yields, decreased tourism and recreation attraction |
| oral mining | coral reef destruction | decreased fish yields, decreased tourism and recreation attraction, increased shoreline erosion |
| oastal or offshore mining | sediment and turbidity, pollution of coral reefs | decreased fish yields, decreased tourism and recreation attraction |
| il shipping along offshore international routes | oil pollution of offshore waters | decreased growth of coral reef, increased beach erosion, decreased tourism attraction |
| redging for construction materials | sediment and turbidity, pollution of coral reefs | decreased fish yields, decreased tourism and recreation attraction |
| op, grazing or forestry practices in coastal atersheds | watershed erosion, sediment and turbidity pollution of coral reefs | decreased fish yields, decreased tourism and recreation attraction |

| USE OR ACTIVITY ——— ——— | → ENVIRONMENTAL CHANGE ——— | → IMPACT OF SOCIAL CONCERN |
|---|---|---|
| fishing with dynamite | coral reef destruction | decreased fish yields, decreased tourism and recreation attraction |
| intensive, localized fishing effort | harvesting at rate greater than sustainable yield | decreased coral reef associated fish yields |
| F. Beach, dune and delta impacts | | |
| recreation and/or tourism development | trampling of beach and dune vegetation | initiation or increase of shoreline erosion, increased hazard, decreased tourism and recreation attraction |
| grazing of livestock | trampling and/or overgrazing of beach and dune stabilizing vegetation | initiation or increase of dune migration onto agricultural areas or infrastructure |
| mining beach sand | removal at rate greater than natural accretion, | initiation or increase of beach shoreline erosion, increased hazard, loss of native vegetation, wildlife habitat and natural amenities, decreased tourism atraction |
| flood control and/or agricultural development and impoundment or diversions of coastal rivers | decreased suply of beach material to shoreline | initiation or increase of shoreline erosion, increased hazard |
| G. Fishing effort | | |
| intensive and extensive fishing effort | harvesting at rate greater than sustainable yield | decreased fish yields |
| competition between onshore and offshore fishermen for same stocks | harvesting at rate greater than sustainable yield | decreased fish yields, social conflicts between groups |

| USE OR ACTIVITY → | ENVIRONMENTAL CHANGE → | IMPACT OF SOCIAL CONCERN |
|---|---|---|
| H. Access to the shorelines and subtidal areas | | |
| residential development on the shoreline, tourism development of shoreline | blocked or impaired public access to the shore | resentment among local inhabitants, increased recreation pressure on accessible areas, site deterioration, decreased recreational quality |
| I. Visual quality | | |
| residential development, tourism development | decreased visual quality of rural or natural landscape | decreased recreation and tourism quality |
| J. Employment and cultural values | | |
| tourism development | increased salaries in tourism sector relative to other sectors, erosion of local customs and cultural values | loss of agricultural workers, decreased agricultural productivity, resentment and social problems among nationals |

## ANNEX 3

### Short description and discussion of some strategies in marine pollution control

#### Water quality standards

In general, regulatory standards on the water quality of effluents and the recipient water bodies have been adopted to meet scientifically derived water quality criteria. Both standards and criteria are determined according to the choice of water quality objectives formulated. The main advantage of the water quality objectives approach is that standards can be set according to the particular uses of water resources. Water quality standards are mainly based on short-term bioassays of acute or lethal effects on test organisms that reside in the water column. The implied assumption is that the major compartment of the aquatic system in which a given substance will accumulate is the water column.

However, when designing or applying pollution control based on water quality standards, it is important to consider that water quality standards:

- are often not up-to-date, since many standards were first established decades ago;
- do not take into account the biogeochemical behaviour of many substances, which primarily accumulate in aquatic sediments;
- do not necessarily apply to species which are most sensitive to a given substance;
- do not reflect risk/effect of a substance accumulated throughout a food chain;
- are often applied ubiquitously to drastically different ecosystems, neglecting a) biogeochemical and ecological differences, b) impact of multiple sources (i.e. overall load), and c) impact of substance in the areas of medium and long-term residence;
- imply analysis of potentially harmful substances in the water column which may be difficult to perform precisely and accurately. Improvements in analytical capacities required can be very costly.

#### Uniform emission standards (UES)

The UES approach sets limits on the effluent concentrations of particular substances concerned. Same limits are applied to all discharges of the substance in question or all processes of a particular type. The limits are usually set in terms of the concentrations allowed in the effluent and, in the case of a particular process, in terms of the amount of product produced. In applying this approach in marine pollution control, black and grey lists of harmful substances are set up and/or requirements for effluent treatment technology are specified.

#### Black and grey lists

Black and grey lists divide substances into two groups according to the degree of their risk/effect characteristics in terms of - either high or low - persistence, toxicity and bioaccumulation potential. Black-listed substances would not be allowed to enter the aquatic environment whereas the less dangerous grey-listed substances may be discharged, subject to certain precautions, which in most cases include effluent treatment requirements. Regarding this approach it is to be considered that:

- there is no clear dividing line between groups;

- local conditions and biogeochemical behaviour are not taken into account (degree of persistence depends on prevailing environmental conditions; significance of both toxicity and bioaccumulation differs according to the target species);

- it ignores particular circumstances that influence the risk the substances actually pose in a real situation.

Best available technology (BAT)

This is a strategy for restricting dissemination of substances and reducing environmental impacts through source reduction using the most refined and effective technology currently available. In many cases, this approach is applied to effluent treatment requirements which would include maximum removal of a given substance, regardless of costs. If economic factors are taken into consideration the level of treatment called for may be less; - an option which is often described as using the "best practicable means available" (BPMA). However, it should be recognized that this approach:

- is not designed for environmental protection on a site-specific basis;

- takes no account either of other sources or the level of environmental protection actually required;

- does not assess whether protection is actually achieved;

- may prove to be totally inadequate or overly protective.

Precautionary principle

The precautionary principle states that precautionary action (e.g., discharge control) should be taken, even without scientific evidence of cause and effect relationships, if the substance is suspected of having detrimental effects on the marine environment. The precautionary principle is frequently being interpreted as a requirement to proceed towards zero discharge for all materials excepting uncontaminated natural substances.

In scientific terms, acceptance of this principle poses fundamental problems. A major criticism of this principle is the acceptance of suspicion of effects rather than scientific evidence as sufficient to introduce discharge controls. As it stands, this principle can be invoked by simply arguing that at some future date a given chemical is likely to have an effect and discharge to the sea should be banned. Since the introduction of most substances to the marine environment will cause at least local disturbances and because effect is not defined, this argument can and is being invoked in relation to most sources of direct inputs to the marine environment. A second problem is that it lacks qualitative and quantitative definitions of the terms persistent, toxic and bioaccumulatable.

Precautionary attitudes should however be adopted in cases where only little is known about a given chemical or its biogeochemical behaviour and ecological risks as well as where concentrations are approaching established environmental quality standards and/or critical loads.

<u>Some remarks</u>

As for the aquaculture - environment context, evidence will grow that aquaculture development planners will have to also be able to advocate, if not select, certain environmental policy approaches in order to meet specific requirements/needs of the very diverse aquaculture practices and the people involved herein. This is not an easy task considering the variety of existing concepts and methodologies for environmental protection all of which have advantages and limitations in their application.

Economic considerations will certainly determine the adoption of an environmental protection strategy. Traditionally-used strategies have the advantage of being relatively easy to organize, administer and monitor, and, often, they do not require detailed investigation of environmental variables, which inevitably vary form site to site. However, it must be recognized, that rigid application of traditional approaches may - in the long-term - not prove to be economic, because they do not take account of the extent to which the environment can assimilate wastes.

Last, an example is given for an adaptive and flexible approach, which would combine advantages of some strategies. As for pollution control of African waters, for which ecotoxicological data are scarce, Biney *et al.* (1987) list following strategy options for the management of polluting discharges.

1) Limitation of the effluent by means of *rigid* effluent standards, both with chemical concentration limits and/or with a toxicological limit derived by simple acute toxicity tests on effluents. However, the specific characteristics of the receiving waterbody are not considered.
2) Limitation of the effluent by *flexible* standards. Here, the limits are calculated in order to maintain water quality criteria in a *specific* waterbody. Also, in this case, the limit can be defined as a threshold of the chemical and/or its toxic effects.
3) For some chemical substances it is scientifically unsound, and insufficient for environmental protection to set up objectives, criteria and regulations for water alone. The classical case is mercury (Moore and Ramamoorthy, 1984). In such cases, it is necessary to indicate objectives or criteria for another environmental compartment (e.g. sediments and/or fish).
4) In some cases, where a species is shown to be particularly sensitive to certain substances (e.g. crustaceans to pesticides), an "indicator-species" - oriented management strategy has to be preferred to the water quality criteria approach (Hellawell, 1986).
5) The classification of chemical substances in use in a country into "black", "grey" and "white" lists can be of help (Hellawell, 1986), especially in the framework of a Hazard Assessment approach to water quality control, i.e.

the comparison of predicted environmental exposure with available toxicity data. This does not necessarily mean that black-listed chemicals are to be totally banned, but that they should be used only under certain conditions and strict controls.

## ANNEX 4

**Overview of aquaculture-specific monitoring parameters and characteristics for which data may be collected:**

- hydrographic and topographic conditions of coastal water bodies in terms of current directions and speeds, tide dynamics, wave actions, winds, retention times of water masses in embayments, stratification patterns, estuarine mixing of marine and fresh water masses, fluctuations in river flows, depth and slope of ground water table; sills, depths, slopes, seabed types, sedimentation and erosion patterns, etc.;

- ecological characteristics of "undisturbed" benthic and pelagic communities as well as of littoral/riparian fauna and flora;

- patterns, extent and consequences of aquatic contamination and physical degradation by coastal activities other than aquaculture;

- location, lifetime and layout of the aquafarm, including size, design/construction of holding units, water supply channels, tubing, pre- and post- water treatment facilities, quality of water supply, water exchange requirements (salt water/fresh water), properties of pond soils, etc.;

- cultured organisms, including type and number of species/strains, size/age, stocking density, growth, (if possible biomass), yield per production cycle; time of stocking and harvesting; disease problems (type, onset, duration), losses (predation, escapements, fall-off, mortalities), etc.;

- inputs, including feeds, fertilizers, chemicals, in terms of type, quantity, composition (if possible, content of water, inorganic and organic carbon, nitrogen, phosphorus) consistency, food particle size; methods, schedule and frequency of feeding, fertilizing and chemical usage;

- spatial and temporal changes in the water column within and/or around the farm, in terms of water circulation/current speeds, salinity, turbidity, colour, temperature, pH, dissolved oxygen, dissolved inorganic nutrients, total carbon, total nitrogen, total phosphorus, suspended and settleable particulate matter, BOD, seston, (chlorophyll, pheopigments), etc.

- spatial and temporal changes in and on the seabed (and pond bottoms) in terms of sediment colour, thickness, consistency, pH, redox potential, organic matter content, BOD, COD, total carbon, total nitrogen, total phosphorus, dissolved inorganic nutrients, dissolved oxygen, hydrogen sulphide, methane, drug residuals, etc.

- spatial and temporal changes in benthic and pelagic organisms (partly including cultured organisms) in terms of responses at biochemical and cellular level, responses at the level of individual organisms (morphological anomalies, reduced reproduction, growth and survival, accumulation of chemicals in tissues), responses at population and community level (abundance of indicator species, species richness, abundance, biomass, diversity), energy flow in food webs, etc.

# ANNEX 5

**Overview of socio-economic parameters which may need to be considered in coastal aquaculture development** (based on Schmidt, 1982)

## A) The need to determine social feasibility of coastal aquaculture.

According to Smith and Pestano-Smith (1985) there is a need to determine social feasibility of coastal aquaculture because of several factors (slightly modified):

- the considerable pace of technological development in some coastal aquaculture systems,
- the expansion of potential export markets for the products of coastal aquaculture and the economic pressure that this potential creates for increased production,
- the need to add to the supply of aquatic protein available domestically,
- the sometimes fragile nature of the coastal areas and the potential effects of increased competition for coastal resources, and
- the lack of institutional preparedness to deal with such extreme competition.

## B) Three basic questions.

Following three basic questions may be relevant when considering the socio-economic circumstances in areas of existing and future coastal aquaculture development:

- Which are the technical and economic parameters which determine the feasibility of coastal aquaculture ?
- Which are the actual needs of the people and/or requirements for a structural improvement of their communities ?
- Which is the potential impact of the innovation of coastal aquaculture with respect to those needs and requirements ?

## C) Parameters.

### i) Demographic and economic parameters

#### 1) Demography

- population, population densities, growth rates;
- distribution of age groups, male-female ratio;
- economically active number of people, male-female ratio;
- average of households, typical composition;
- migration trends;
- ratio of urban/rural population;
- ethnic composition.

#### 2) Infrastructure

- transport and communications within the area, transport and communication links with other areas, and transport and communication centres;
- availability of electricity and water;

- existing market channels;
- services such as schools, dispensaries, hospitals, etc.

3) Sector analysis of the local economy

The analysis will investigate the different sectors of an economy, usually dividing it into: (a) a primary sector as agriculture, fisheries, forestry, mining, etc., (b) a secondary sector as industry and manufacture, and (c) a tertiary sector as services, trade, tourism, etc. For each sector, the analysis will briefly examine the following:

- production structure and magnitude;
- demand, supply price structure;
- input-output dynamics;
- ownership of means of production;
- employment structure and relative wages;
- investment trends and potentials;
- marketing;
- constraints to expansion and growth.

4) Income distribution

- income per household and per caput in cash and kind;
- seasonality of incomes;
- ratio of income earners/dependent household members;
- percentages of income generated by subsistence production, market production, wage labour;
- relation of incomes to the national average and the GDP per caput.

5) Household expenditures and consumption patterns

- percentage and items acquired by purchase, barter, or self-production;
- expenditure by items;
- seasonal variations of expenditures.

ii) Social dynamics and variables

- legal and normative structures;
- traditional and modern institutions, their role and function;
- structure of leadership: traditional and religious, political and economic, their interdependence;
- social sub-organizations, their status, interactions and transparency;
- decision-making on the community level;
- social control mechanisms, norms and values.

iii) Socio-cultural variables

- cultural and religious identity of the individual and nucleus-groups;
- self-assessment, expectations;
- mobility (occupational, geographical, vertical) and participation;
- value patterns and attitudinal preconceptions;
- role and status of individuals and nucleus groups;
- socialization and its determinants;
- decision-making at the family level.

## ANNEX 6

### Some examples of EIA sequences

### 1. ODA (1988) :

- initial screening (IS)
  - registers danger signals
  - avoids unnecessary investigations where impacts likely to be minimal

- environmental appraisal (EA)
  - predicts main impacts
  - assesses importance of effects
  - indicates key mitigating actions required
  - presents implications to decision-makers

- environmental impact assessment (EIA)
  - predicts in detail likely impacts, including cost implications
  - identifies specific measures necessary to avoid, mitigate or compensate for damage
  - presents predictions and options to decision-makers

- monitoring & evaluation (feedback mechanism)
  - indicates additional mitigating actions required
  - improves IS, EA and EIA
  - increases knowledge base of environmental effects

### 2. UNEP (1988) :

- screening
- preliminary assessment
- organisation of EIA study
- scoping
- EIA study

  identification<br>
  prediction<br>
  evaluation<br>
  mitigation<br>
  documentation

using the results: decision-maker: plan for reducing conflicts; allocating institutional responsibilities; post-auditing

3. Ahmad and Sammy (1985) :

- preliminary activities
- impact identification (scoping)
- baseline study
- impact evaluation (quantification)
- mitigation measures
- assessment (comparison of alternatives)
- documentation
- decision making
- post auditing

4. Bisset (1983) :

- impact identification
- impact prediction and measurement
- impact interpretation or evaluation
- identification of monitoring requirements and mitigating measures
- communication of impact information to users (decision-makers; public)

5. Lohani and Halim (1983) :

- identification
  - description of the existing environmental system
  - determination of the components of the project

- prediction
  - identification of the environmental modification that may be significant
  - forecasting of the quantity and/or spatial dimension of change in the environment identified

- evaluation
  - determination of the incidence of cost and benefit to user groups and population affected by the project
  - specification and comparison of the trade-offs (costs or effects being balanced) between various alternatives

# ANNEX 7

## Some considerations in the formulation of programmes for ICAM
(adapted from Clark, 1991)

1. Recognize and treat the coastal area as a dynamic system, and the demands on the coastal area as dynamic.

2. The planning horizon must be longer than the five years typically used, perhaps several decades or more, for example, for issues of shoreline erosion and sea level rise. Economic and technological developments should be projected, under alternative scenarios, for 10-20 years.

3. The principal functions of ecosystems should be sustained.

4. Use an environmental and resource assessment as the basis for comprehensive land use planning. describe functions that must be served. Do environmental and resource assessment up front. Make a series of forecasts.

5. Fit coastal land and water uses in where they make sense. Weigh existing development and its attendant demands for liquid and solid wastes disposal and hence pollution impacts; identify and develop means for managing point and non-point sources of pollution.

6. Tailor guidelines to the existing level of development.

7. Establish a working definition of "environmental quality" beyond pollution abatement.

8. Emphasize occurrence of natural processes. Recognize that current status of any given natural system is not fixed; it may represent a dynamic equilibrium or a transitional system.

9. Encourage enhancement and restoration of ecosystems; take advantage of natural processes; encourage proper siting.

10. Examples of functions (outputs) for ICAM include, but are not limited to:

    - Production function (fish, seagrass, drinking water, sand and shells, nutrients, water for cooling systems)
    - Support functions (physical space: areas for settlement, beaches, recreation, shipping routes, harbors)
    - Regulation functions (organic matter, storm water, erosion buffering)
    - Information functions (scientific studies, bird watching, genetic functions)
    - Ethical and aesthetic (existence value)

11. As a rule, short-term economic considerations fuel political priorities.

12. Analytical techniques of economic valuation are being improved. Although not providing the final answers, these techniques do provide information useful for resource management decisions.

13. No ICAM programme yet exists as a working model. The information needs and concepts required for defining the objectives of ICAM are still being developed. The subject matter is extremely diverse and the framework for training and education is being developed.

# ANNEX 8

## Some principal types of information needed for ICAM
(adapted from Clark, 1991)

**1. Physical environment:**

terrain data (including history), erosional processes, storm surge, winds, tides, air-sea interaction, sediment transport, geological setting, subsidence, sediment supply, meteorology, climate.

**2. Biological environment:**

primary and secondary production, distribution and extent of living coastal resources, major habitats and ecosystems, ecological relationships that determine productivity, presence of rare, threatened or endangered species; indicator species.

**3. Sociological information:**

resource dependency, historic use patterns including methods, factors determining historic use patterns, current use patterns, identify whether current use patterns are sustainable, demography, socio-cultural information, land and sea tenure.

**4. Economics:**

resource and resource use patterns should be given economic values. Qualitative values - resource and resource use patterns that cannot be economically valued should be considered. Some specific economic pursuits that should be included in data collection are: fisheries, aquaculture, forestry, agriculture, settlements, tourism, extractive and manufacturing industries, energy, waste disposal and treatment, transportation, ports, traditional practices.

**5. Issues:**

it is necessary to identify the groups with a stake in the use and management of coastal resources and potential conflicts among them.

**6. Institutional mechanisms:**

(national, state, and local) ministries, departments with division of responsibility, organization and hierarchy; interagency councils, advisory panels, standing agreements with private parties; legislation on zoning, pollution, resources, utilization; permitting and other administrative processes to carry out legislation.

# ANNEX 9

**Premises and considerations for a management strategy in ICAM**
(adapted from Clark, 1991)

- Not all countries need ICAM in the formal sense.
- While conservation of renewable resources may be a main purpose of ICAM, economic development is the theme.
- Specially protected areas may be an integral part of an ICAM programme.
- There is not a generic working model of ICAM presently known.
- Access to information must be assured.
- A linkage to key policy-makers must be established.
- There should be linkages between complementary government offices and agencies.
- Attempts to bring together diverse interest groups must be made.
- Tools must be devised to translate technical information into workable management information.
- Information should be disseminated to policy-makers, various parties at interest, and the public.
- A constituency for ICAM must be built to sustain the management activity.

# ANNEX 10

## A proposed code of practice for the use of inhibitory compounds in aquaculture
(from GESAMP, 1991c)

1. Medically important inhibitory coumpounds should be banned from use in aquaculture. However, some medically important compounds may need to be used in exceptional circumstances for certain specified diseases.

2. The availability of inhibitory compounds should be restricted to qualified individuals, such as veterinarians.

3. Access to inhibitory compounds should be denied to all laymen and inexperienced personnel.

4. The storage of inhibitory compounds should be in the manner recommended by manufacturers/suppliers.

5. The use of inhibitory compounds should be strictly in accordance with the written instructions from the manufacturer/supplier.

6. The use of pharmaceutical compounds should be by rotation. Thus, the repeated use of single compounds should be avoided.

7. The use of suitable withdrawal periods, after the use of pharmaceutical compounds, is necessary before animals are removed from the aquacultural facility.

8. The deliberate or accidental release of inhibitory compounds into the aquatic environment must be avoided.

9. Unused inhibitory compounds must be disposed off safely.

10. A surveillance programme must be adopted to ensure that the code of practice is carried out.

# ANNEX 11

## A checklist on projects for coastal aquaculture development
(modified from Burb:idge *et al.*, 1988)

| Important issues | Quality of information: | | | | | |
|---|---|---|---|---|---|---|
| | Available | | Current | | Reliable | |
| | Yes | No | Yes | No | Yes | No |
| 1. What is the principle method of culture proposed (ponds, floating cage or raft, bottom culture, pens)? Specify reasons for method(s) selected. | | | | | | |
| 2. Will this be based upon extensive or intensive production? Assess availability/affordability of resources required. | | | | | | |
| 3. If the proposal is for extensive production, has the improvement of the efficiency of existing aquaculture been explored as an alternative means of supporting increased coastal population and increased fishery production? | | | | | | |
| 4. Will the land or water areas required involve the clearance of mangrove, tidal swamp forest, agricultural land or other uses? Describe alternatives for project location. | | | | | | |
| 5. Has the impact on these areas and/or uses been examined? Specify publics or communities interested or affected by the project. | | | | | | |
| 6. Is the proposed location for the project capable of sustaining aquaculture on a long term basis? Specify limitations/constraints. | | | | | | |
| 7. Will the development affect resources which form the basis of other fishery activities (for example-quality of water entering adjacent mangrove areas, sea grass beds, coral reefs)? Specify extent and severity of potential effects. | | | | | | |
| 8. Will the development affect resources which form the basis of other activities inland (for example will the creation of brackish water ponds increase soil salinity in adjacent agricultural areas)? Specify extent and severity of potential effects. | | | | | | |
| 9. Will the project be located in an area subject to natural hazards including riverine flooding tsunami(tidal waves), hurricanes, typhoons or storm surges? | | | | | | |
| 10. Is the location subject to potential man made hazards including industrial, thermal or agricultural pollution? Specify risks involved. | | | | | | |
| 11. Are there human health hazards associated with the proposed location? | | | | | | |
| 12. Will the project increase the occurrence of water-borne diseases? | | | | | | |

The figures and tables as well as annex 1, as listed below, were included in this document with kind permission, as required, by following publishers and institutions:

Figures 5 and 6. From Gowen and Bradbury, 1987. Oceanogr.Mar.Biol.Annu.Rev., 25:563-575. (Figure 1 on page 566; Figure 2 on page 569).

© *Aberdeen University Press Ltd.*

Figure 7. From Chua *et al.*, 1989. Mar.Pollut.Bull., 20(7):335-343. (Figure 3 on page 339).

© *Maxwell Pergamon Macmillan plc.*

Figure 9. From Gowen *et al.*, 1990. In Aquaculture Europe '89 - Business joins science, edited by N. De Pauw and R. Billard. Bredene, European Aquaculture Society. EAS Special Publication No. 12, pp.257-283. (Figure 2 on page 260).

© *European Aquaculture Society.*

Figure 11. From Wallin and Hakanson, 1991. In Marine Aquaculture and Environment. edited by T. Makinen. Copenhagen, Nordic Council of Ministers. Nord 1991(22): pp.39-55. (Figure 3 on page 45).

© *Nordic Council of Ministers.*

Figure 12. From Gowen *et al.*, 1989. In Aquaculture - A biotechnology in progress. Proceedings of the International Conference Aquaculture Europe '87, held 2-5 June 1987 in Amsterdam, The Netherlands, edited by N. De Pauw, E. Jaspers, H. Ackefors and N. Wilkins. Bredene, European Aquaculture Society. Vol.2, pp.1071-1080. (Figure 2 on page 1074).

© *European Aquaculture Society.*

Figure 13. From Weston, 1991. In Aquaculture and water quality, edited by D.E. Brune and J.R. Tomasso. Baton Rouge, World Aquaculture Society. Advances in World Aquaculture, (3), pp.534-567. (Figure 1 on page 539).

© *World Aquaculture Society.*

Figure 14. From Bailly, 1989. In Aquaculture: A review of recent experience. Paris, Organization for Economic Cooperation and Development (OECD), pp.314-327. (Figure 2 on page 318).

© *Organization for Economic Cooperation and Development (OECD).*

Figures 15 and 16. From Driver and Bisset, 1989. In Report of workshops on environmental impact assessment, held in Pakistan, 16 September - 2 October 1989. Environment and Urban Affairs Division of the Government of Pakistan and IUCN-The World Conservation Union. Karachi, JRC-IUCN Pakistan, pp.5-11. (Figure 1 on page 7; Annex IV: Visual Aids; Figure on page 45).

© *JRC - IUCN Pakistan.*

Table 9. From Beveridge *et al.*, 1991. In Aquaculture and water quality, edited by D.E. Brune and J.R. Tomasso. Baton Rouge, World Aquaculture Society. Advances in World Aquaculture, (3), pp.506-533. (Table 6 on page 518).

© *World Aquaculture Society.*

Tables 12 and 13. From Huguenin and Colt, 1989. Design and operating guide for aquaculture seawater systems. Amsterdam, Elsevier Science Publishers. Developments in Aquaculture and Fisheries Science, (20), 264p. (Table 2.3 on page 14; Table 3.1 on page 32).

© *Elsevier Science Publishers B.V.*

Table 14. From Carpenter and Maragos, 1989. How to assess environmental impacts on tropical islands and coastal areas. A training manual prepared for the South Pacific Regional Environment Programme (SPREP). Honolulu, East-West Center, 345p. (Table I.2. on page 12).

© *Environment and Policy Institute, East-West Center.*

Annex 1. From Lin, 1989. World Aquacult., 20(2):19-20. (Article on pages 19-20).

© *World Aquaculture Society.*